Dividend Investing

How to Build Your PASSIVE INCOME and FINANCIAL FREEDOM Through the Stock Market. A Guide to Dividend Stocks and an Early Retirement

James Johnson

Table of Contents

Introduction

Welcome to the era of super low-interest rates!

Probably ever since the beginning of finance, people relied on banks and bond payments to make money from interest. This is called income investing, and for many ordinary people, having money in a savings account that paid good interest was one of the few ways that they could grow their wealth. In the mid to late 20th century, nearly every middle-class household had a savings account in the bank and conservative investors bought high-interest rate products that were safe like CDs.

Unfortunately, because of a lot of factors including bad decisions by the Federal Reserve and the housing crash, times have really changed. We've now had two decades of incredibly low-interest rates by historical standards. They are so low that your money is basically wiped out by the modest inflation we have. You'd be better off putting it in a mattress than buying a money market fund.

While years ago you could make 6% or 7% interest from multiple investments, and put your money in lucrative and very safe products from banks like CDs, today, those same investments only pay 1 to 2%. What a joke! This has left many people struggling, looking for another way to make a safe income from investments. Many people are leery about putting their entire life savings into the stock market, where it could crash and lose most of its value and not recover in time for retirement.

Unfortunately, over those same years, people have also developed bad savings habits. Recent surveys have shown that the majority of Americans could not even pay $500 cash to cover the smallest of emergencies.

Since you've decided to read this book, I can only assume that you have other ideas for your money. At the very least, I have to congratulate you for thinking about what you can do to increase not only your wealth but also your income.

In this book, we are going to take a look at one of the safest ways you can increase your income, while still utilizing the stock market. Over the past 20 years, the stock market has been growing in leaps and bounds, even including the 2008 financial crash and the major recession after the dot com bust. As they say, the rich get richer, and as interest rates continue to drop, money kept flowing into the stock market.

Of course, the stock market has also been driven by technological changes such as the advent of the Internet, smartphones, the gig economy, and innovative companies like Netflix and Tesla. But the fact remains that a lot of money is going into the stock market in part because interest rates are so low.

Another safe investment that people used to rely on a great deal were bonds purchased from the United States government. Now, money is continuing to flow into those bonds, but for the ordinary person, they don't offer the value that they once did. Interest rates are ridiculously low on the treasury issued by the United States government. They do have an inflation-protected option, but the amount of interest you would earn on the US government bond pales in comparison to what it would've paid in the 1990s or earlier.

So, in this book, we're going to explore a path that is going to be safe and lucrative for most investors. It's going to take time to build it up, but if you do have a lot of capital to invest right now, you've got a Headstart. Even if you don't have a huge amount of capital, any amount you can start investing in the plans described in this book is going to go along way towards securing your future. Despite the low interest rates, there is still a way that you can earn passive income off of investments and it's relatively safe.

Of course, we are talking about dividends. Many large companies that are relatively stable still pay good dividend payments. For those who are new to the subject, a dividend is a *cash payment* that the company will pay out of their profits every quarter to stockholders. Payments are calculated on a per share basis.

So, to build your passive income over time, all you need to do is purchase shares on a regular basis. Of course, you have to know the right companies to invest in and all the issues associated with dividends, and what dividend investing entails. We hope to answer all those questions for you in this book. So, let's go ahead and get started!

Chapter 1

Overview and Advantages of

Dividend Investing

In today's world, we all have a sense that we need to grow our money. Many people would also like a source of passive income and a way to add to their income in retirement. Living off Social Security isn't really an option for any quality-of-life. Unfortunately, far too many depend only on Social Security. It wasn't that long ago when people could rely on FDIC insured banks to not only grow their money but also to act as a source of passive income. Bonds, which are basically loans that a private individual makes either to a government entity or to a corporation, also used to be a reliable way to earn interest payments off of your money. Back in the days when you could earn 6 to 10% interest from bonds, it was a very safe and lucrative way to earn money. It's hard to believe that in 1990, which really wasn't that long ago, you could actually buy US treasuries and earn solid money off of them every six months. You also have the guarantee of safety for your principal that was in the hands of the United States government. Of course, today, the government is in massive debt and the debt continues to grow. Now, the government is actually threatened by rising interest rates. Already, paying interest is practically becoming as large a part of the budget as the defense budget is. Can you imagine a world in which the government is paying more money for interest on its debt than it is for national security? That is a pretty crazy situation.

So, as we alluded to in the introduction, there is still a safe way that investors can protect their principal at least to a certain degree and also earn a passive income. This is by investing in dividend stocks.

There are different ways that you could do this, but one way that provides the remarkable benefits of growth that the stock market can provide, with at least a certain degree of safety, is to invest in solid companies with growing dividend payments. Later in the chapter, we are going to look at a few companies that serve as examples. But before we get into that, let's explain what dividends are and how they work for people who are beginners when it comes to the subject of dividend investing.

A basic overview of what dividends are

So, first things first. Right now, the stock market continues to provide a way that you can grow your money at a pace that is faster than inflation. Many people are understandably leery of the stock market because they lived through at least the 2008 financial crisis, and many others are old enough to remember both the recession after the 9/11 terrorist attacks and the dot com recession that happened in the late 1990s. You also don't have to be that old to remember black Tuesday in 1987. So many people have a misperception of the stock market-based in part on those crashes and also based on the misperception that the stock market is a gambling casino. Now, of course, if you approach it that way, the stock market could be a gambling casino. And many people do approaches this way by engaging in speculation such as day trading stocks in an effort to earn fast profits. We won't get into that here, but it goes without saying that most people are not disciplined enough to make money from those kinds of activities. The reality is most people trying to make quick cash in the stock market. But the fact that many people do succeed at such activities always keeps those dreams of making fast money in a day or two alive.

Of course, if you're interested in dividends, you are a more realistic and sensible person when it comes to handling money. You realize that investment and not speculation is the time-tested and true way to grow your money over the long-term. The fact is the long-term investors who buy-and-hold and don't panic always come out ahead.

The great depression and the 2008 financial crisis both illustrate why it is stupid to panic and pull your money out of the stock market during downturns. Let's take a look at the 2008 crash first. For our benchmark, we'll just use the Dow Jones industrial average. Although it's not the best benchmark probably, the valley of the Dow is what most people associate with the stock market, and of course, it does track with all the other indices.

According to the St. Louis Federal Reserve Bank, on July 10, 2009, the Dow Jones industrial average was 8146. Two years later, it was already over 12,000. The market had already grown by about 54% at that time. By the time Pres. Obama was about to leave office in late December 2016, the Dow Jones industrial average was about 19,700 points. So, since that first date we quoted, the stock market had basically grown about 142%.

Now, those are some returns. Hopefully, our readers are aware that you can buy index funds that track major stock market indices. So, imagine what you're money could've done investing just in the Dow Jones industrial average over that time span.

Now, of course, we are not trying to peddle the idea that this kind of growth is always going to happen. The point of this exercise is only to illustrate that recessions, even major ones, are temporary events. The overall growth of the economy and the capital in the economy is something that is a constant growth factor, and that's been proven over a very long period of time.

So, we can even see this in the mother of all recessions, the great depression of the 1930s. In July 1929, the stock market was experiencing an unprecedented rise in value. It was nearing the 5000-mark at that time. That is pretty incredible given that the economy was much smaller back then. By the summer of 1932, the market has dropped all the way down to about 842 points. Now, that seems pretty dismal and it definitely was. There were many factors that led to this; one of the most important was the Smoot-

Hawley tariff act, which nearly single-handedly killed global trade. The Federal Reserve, which at that time had only been around for about 15 or 16 years, really didn't know how to handle the crisis. So, another factor that kept the depression going and worsened its effects is that the Federal Reserve severely reduced the money supply. Had these two events not happened to, add to the stock market crash, the Great Depression would've been much milder.

Those issues are for a discussion on another day. What's important for us is that from 1932 onwards, even though it was still a very difficult decade which included the rise of Adolf Hitler and Japan launching wars across Asia, the stock market experience great rebounds after 1932. Four years after Franklin Delano Roosevelt had been elected; the stock market had risen by 236%. Now, of course, I wasn't alive in 1932, but if you would have advised people in the summer of 1932 that the best thing they could do was to invest in the stock market, they would've thought you were completely crazy. And yet those people that did invest would have seen absolutely amazing returns.

We don't want to get too caught up in this, the point you should take away from this is that even the most drastic shocks to the stock market are temporary and are followed by great rebounds.

Another thing to consider is that things don't grind to a complete halt during economic downturns. For those who have lost their jobs, if they don't have any life savings, of course, an economic downturn is a major crisis. And yet, there are still massive amounts of economic activity going on. Even during the depression when unemployment rates reached record levels, most people were still employed. The same holds true for the 2008 financial crisis. If you avoid the temptation of looking at the size of the economy in relative terms comparing it to just a few years earlier which is what a recession actually does and look at it in absolute terms, even in the depths of the 2008 financial crisis, the United States economy was absolutely huge. Don't get me wrong, I'm not trying to downplay the huge problems that there were and the necessity to deal with them. But remember this. Even during an economic downturn, people need to get their prescription drugs, they still watch television, they are still using electricity, and they're still buying basic goods like toilet paper and food. So, here's a hint. A company like Walgreens which is an old established company based on providing vital daily goods is well-placed to survive an economic crisis.

All right, we spent enough time on this detour. But I hope that for those who are leery of the stock market, that is an objective review of some of the data makes them feel a little bit more relaxed about placing their money in the stock market. In the next section, I'm going to go over a couple of general strategies that will help you avoid getting financially destroyed by the fortunes of one single company or a single sector of the economy.

The Importance of Diversification

One of the most important strategies any investor in the stock market can use is diversification. Many people understand this to mean that you will take your money and put it in maybe 20 stocks or something like that. That kind of gets the idea. However, it doesn't go nearly far enough. In the next chapter, we are going to talk about diversification in detail. But I don't mind mentioning it multiple times because it's so important. So, let me say this, putting your stock in 20 different companies is the bare minimum that you want to do in order to protect your capital. These days, we're only left with the choices of protecting our capital in nominal value by putting it in a bank or investing in bonds, contrasted with putting it at risk in the stock market. I think, by now, you're convinced that putting your capital in the bank or in bonds is something a little more attractive than bearing it in your backyard. With that in mind, that means we need a strategy where we can protect our money by taking advantage of the growth of the stock market.

And, of course, a major theme of this book, is actually also to take advantage of dividend payments for income, and moreover, seeking dividend payments that are growth-oriented. So, in the end, you really don't need a bank account except for emergency savings. And let me do my duty at this point and encourage you to put a great deal of effort into building a small savings account to help you weather problems that may arise in your life. If you don't have a savings account or if you do and there's hardly any money in it, I recommend that you make a goal of getting $20,000 into that savings account. Now, you don't have to do that all at once, but set a goal that is at most 24-36 months out, to put regular monthly deposits into your savings account. After that, just leave it alone, unless it's a true emergency.

A Brief Look at Compound Interest

Anytime that you learn something new, you need to become familiar with the definitions of that niche or industry. First of all, let's recognize that dividend investing really has two goals.

The first goal is to leverage the stock market and the capital appreciation that it provides in order to grow our wealth over time. Many large and stable companies are obviously not going to be growing as fast as the hottest new stocks like Amazon, Netflix, or Google. However, they are going to be growing and probably much faster than inflation. When it comes to the stock market, many people have a shortsighted viewpoint. They have a Time window in mind that is short-term and so they are always looking at the ups and downs that take place over a year or two or even day-to-day. But that is not the correct way to look at it if you are a serious investor. You need to look at what happens to your money over long time frames. So, let's consider a 23-year time period to see what actually happened to Walgreens stock prices. For the record, Walgreens isn't exactly the best stock. But in 1996, it was about eight dollars a share. At the time that I am writing this, Walgreens is about $30 a share. So, its value has grown by 275%. If you had bought $10,000 worth of shares in 1996, you would have about 1,250 shares that would be worth $37,500 today. And we are imagining that you just bought the shares and didn't keep investing.

If you're going to compare that too what would happen to your money in a bank, you're going to find that the bank is hardly worth anything at all in comparison. Let's use a 20-year United States Treasury bond as an example of current interest rates. Right now, according to the St. Louis Federal Reserve Bank, the interest rate on a 20-year treasury bond is 2.8%. If you invested $10,000 into something that had an interest rate of 2.8% that was constant, after 20 years, you would have a little more than $17,000. That's a lot less than you would have by buying stock in Walgreens. So, here is a graph that I created at Smart asset.com showing how your money would've grown if you invested $10,000 into something that paid 2.8% interest and assuming you put no additional money:

To be completely honest, I'm not sure why anyone would even consider this. Inflation is going to wipe out all of your gains. Now, of course, having $17,372 in the year 2038 would be a little better than going into your backyard and digging out the original $10,000, which we assume you protected by putting in a treasure chest. But if you were putting your money into Walgreens, as crazy as it sounds, you would be far better off. And we haven't even considered the fact that Walgreens pays dividends on top of the growth that it experiences in the stock market. And probably more to the point, there are many stocks that you can choose that are far better than Walgreens.

What is a Dividend?

So, now, let's turn our attention more directly to the topic of the book. The first thing we should make sure that everyone understands is what a dividend is. Simply put, a dividend is a share of the profits of the company for the previous quarter paid to stockholders in cash. The share that you're provided is obviously proportional to the number of shares of stock in the company that you own. Typically, the amount of the dividend is calculated as a percentage per share. Dividends are paid out on a quarterly basis. As we will see later, you can earn dividend income buying individual stocks or by buying into a fund like an exchange-traded fund. A great approach to investing is to have a portfolio that contains a little bit of both. As far as mutual funds, there is no reason to invest in mutual funds anymore. Mutual funds have a strict disadvantage in the high fees that they charge and the fact that they only trade once per day after hours. Exchange-traded funds give you all the benefits of mutual funds but without all the hassles and expensive fees. They trade just like stocks so you can buy and sell them at will on your own.

Please be aware that some companies pay dividends in shares of stock rather than cash. Of course, you can choose to keep the extra shares as a form of reinvestment, or if you are looking to make cash you can sell them for the profits.

Ex-dividend Date

The ex-dividend date is an important date that you need to know about if you are investing in stocks that pay dividends. The first thing you need to know is that the ex-dividend date is a cut-off date that is used to determine who will receive a dividend payment on a stock. In order to receive the dividend payment, you must own the shares of stock before the ex-dividend date. If you buy the shares of stock on or after the ex-dividend date, the seller of the shares will receive the dividend payment. This is also called the ex-date.

Date of Record

The date of record is that date at which a company will determine who is eligible to receive a dividend payment. People who own shares of stock two days before the date of record are eligible to receive the dividend payments.

So, let's suppose that on September 16, 2019, some hypothetical company announces that it will pay a dividend on October 1, 2019. The date at which it will determine which shareholders of record will be eligible for the dividend payment. For the sake of example, say that the company announces that shareholders "of record on the company's books" on September 23, 2019 will be eligible for the dividend. That means that the date of record is September 23. I picked that date for an example because it's a Monday. The ex-dividend date is going to be one day before the date of record, but it is one business day. So that means the ex-dividend date, in this case, will be the previous Friday, which is September 20, 2019. In order to be eligible for the dividend payment, you would have to pay on the shares before September 20, 2019. So, if you bought the shares on September 19, you would receive the dividend payment. But if you bought the shares on September 20, you would not receive the dividend payment, but the person who sold them to you would be the one who receives the dividend.

The date the announcement was made which in our case is September 16, it is called the declaration date.

The ex-dividend date can be looked up on any website that provides information for stock tickers. For example, you can use the free website, Yahoo Finance, to get this information. Of course, the next ex-dividend date won't be available until the company announces it, so it might list the most recent ex-dividend date. As a smart investor, you should buy your shares well before the ex-dividend date.

While the ex-dividend date won't necessarily be listed as current, you can find stocks that pay dividends to see if they have one listed or if it says N/A meaning not applicable.

When are dividends paid

Typically, dividends are paid on a quarterly basis, in January, April, July, and October.

Dividend Yield

In order to find good stocks to invest in one of the characteristics that you're going to look at as a dividend investor is the dividend yield. This is given as a percentage which is why the term yield is used. The dividend yield is the percentage of the current share price that determines the amount of cash per share that is paid out each quarter. Of course, day to day, this value is fluctuating, but you can look at it to get an idea of how much money you can make. To know a value close to the exact amount, you'll want to be checking these numbers on the date that they announced that they will be paying the dividend. But mostly, check a few examples to get an idea of what you're looking at.

While dividends are paid out on a quarterly basis, note that dividend yield is calculated based on annual payments. The formula is:

Dividend yield = (Annual Dividend)/Share price

The way that annual dividend is calculated varies. Sometimes, the annual dividend is the dividend paid by the company over the past fiscal year.

Yield is basically a measure of ROI or return on investment. That is it tells us how much return the investor gets for every dollar invested. Of course, when you look up a company on say, Yahoo Finance, they are going to give you the calculated yield using the current share price, which may be quite a bit different than the share price that you paid to invest in the company.

The dividend yield is heavily influenced by changes in share prices as well. You can see that the yield will go down if share prices rise, while it will increase as share prices decline.

Advantages of Dividend Investing

Investors who are looking for a way to earn a passive annual income will benefit the most from dividend investing. This is the closest you're going to get to earning interest on a savings account which amounted to a significant amount of money that you would have in the old days. If you choose your investments wisely, it's a relatively safe way to invest in the stock market as well, since companies that pay dividends tend to be older and more solid.

You're also looking at the stock market in true investment terms rather than hoping for the excitement you might get from buying and selling shares to make fast profits.

People are always looking for ways to earn passive income. You could try starting an online business to earn passive income, and that might work faster in the event that you succeed, but the reality is most online businesses end up going nowhere or losing money. Depending on how much capital you have available, you can start earning a passive income right now from dividend stocks that are pretty much automatic. Generally, since you're probably not a zillionaire already, it's going to take longer for you to earn income from dividend stocks, but over the long term, it's also far more solid.

Two ways to potentially realize gains

If you buy shares in a new company that doesn't pay dividends, you're only able to realize gains from the price appreciation of the shares. You're hoping to buy low and sell high at some point. However, while you have an ownership stake in the company, your profits are locked in. During the time that you own shares, you can't realize any of the profits to require you to sell. With dividend stocks, however, you are earning money off the shares themselves, while you hold them. However, you're also gaining wealth from the price appreciation of the shares, if it's a good stock. So, you gain from asset appreciation the way you would in owning shares in a company that doesn't pay dividends but you're also getting an income from the dividend payments in the meantime.

Newer companies don't pay dividends

Paying dividends is giving the stockholders a share of the quarterly profits. Mature companies with stable cash flow can afford to do this, but newer companies that are looking for rapid growth can't. A company that is looking for rapid growth is going to reinvest its profits back into the company rather than pay them out. Of course, mature companies aren't going to pay all their profits out as dividends. They are probably going to reinvest a portion of their profits in their operations as well, but they aren't looking for the kind of rapid expansion a new company is looking for.

Relatively low risk

Most of the stocks you are going to buy as dividend investments are going to be companies that are solid for a very long time. While it's true they may not be quite as dominant ten, twenty, or thirty years from now as they are at the present time, companies that pay dividends tend to have a solid long term outlook. You are going to care about the earning potential from the dividends far more than you are about whether the company is undergoing massive stock appreciation and disrupting its markets. Also consider that you can be moving your investments around as conditions warrant, so you can sell stocks that become less attractive and invest in new ones with better prospects. As we'll see, you can also do very well by investing in funds that hold large numbers of dividend-paying companies.

Types of Dividend Investments

Let's briefly look at the types of dividend investments you can make. We will look in more detail at each of these in the book.

- High Yield Strategy: this type of investment strategy is used if you're looking to obtain the maximum dividends (i.e. income) now. When you use a high yield strategy, you'll be investing in slow growth companies that pay high dividends.

- Growth rate strategy: If you adopt this strategy, you're looking more toward the future, so you'll invest in companies that might be paying lower dividend yields now, but they are experiencing higher than average growth. A company that pays dividends but has a low yield might be in that position because the company is rapidly expanding and trading with a high price to earnings ratio. This is a buy-and-hold strategy that is suitable for investors looking to earn most of your profits from dividends in the future. Of course, if the company is paying dividends, you are going to earn some money now even though it's not as much as you could be earning from high yield, slow growth companies or from your investment in the future, assuming it works out.

- REIT: This is a real estate investment trust. They trade on stock markets and are income-producing investments.

- MLP: This is a master limited partnership, which is an LLC that is publicly traded. As an investor, you are a limited partner in an MLP, and not involved in the actual operation of the company. You will receive quarterly distributions of profits proportional to your ownership stake.

- BDC: This is another less conventional way to earn quarterly profits, BDC means Business Development Company. A BDC is an entity that invests in small to midsized businesses. This provides you a way to earn profits from smaller companies, and it's often described as a venture capital fund that is open to all investors, rather than being closed the way a venture capital fund is. A BDC essentially acts as a pass-through entity, so the profits are passed through to the investors. You can invest in a BDC on stock exchanges, and they can pay handsome yields. However, this is a higher risk type of investment.

Finding Companies that Pay Dividends

Finding companies that pay dividends is easy. You can just look on your brokerage site or use a free site like Yahoo Finance. Look to see if the company has a dividend yield and ex-dividend date listed. This will tell you if the company pays dividends. Yahoo Finance lists the Forward Dividend, which is an estimate of what the future dividend payment per share is going to be. Keep in mind that is an estimate and also keep in mind it's a short term estimate. But it can give you some idea of what your earnings per share would be. Dividends are quoted on an annual basis but you get paid quarterly. So, if you see a dividend of $2.00 per share, that would mean you get a payment of $0.50 per quarter and the quoted value is subject to constant change.

Chapter 2

Figuring Out Income from Dividend Payments

In this chapter, we are going to take a close look at how much income you actually make from dividend payments. We will go over some formal definitions and concepts and then use some specific examples, and look at how different investment strategies can impact your earnings both now and over the long-term. Note that when you are reading company data that has the amount of the dividend in dollars paid per share, you have to be aware as to whether they are discussing the annual basis or quarterly basis. Most of the time, the annual payment is listed.

Determining dividend payments
from Income Statements

In order to determine the dividend payment a company is making, you need the income statement and beginning and end balance sheets. What we need to know are the net income (profit or loss) and retained earnings. When we say retained earnings, this is the cash reserves on hand for the company. Retained earnings are given by cumulative net income minus cumulative dividends, so the difference between net income and the change in retained earnings will tell us the amount of money that the company paid out in dividends.

Dividend payment = net income – change in retained earnings

So, the change in retained earnings is the amount the company didn't pay out in dividends, so its money reinvested into the company, for new plants, equipment, R &D, or whatever the company chooses to spend its money on in order to generate continued growth. If net income is equal to the change in retained earnings, then no dividends were paid out.

Dividend Payout Ratio

One indicator you'll want to pay attention to is the fraction of profits that a company is paying out in dividends. You actually don't want it to be too high, because that doesn't leave much wiggle room if the company needs to reinvest more of their earnings into company operations or if earnings start dropping. With all things being equal, if the company needed to do so, that could mean a smaller dividend payment to your account.

Dividend Payout Ratio = (total dividend payment)/ (net income)

Investors also talk about the retention ratio, which is a measurement of how much cash the company retains. This can be found using the relationship:

Retention Ratio = 1 – Dividend Payout Ratio

Growth-oriented companies are going to have a low dividend payout ratio. This is because they are reinvesting most of their earnings (or often all of their earnings, many growing companies like Netflix pay no dividends at all). Older companies are not expected to be as aggressive for growth, and so they tend to have higher dividend payout ratios.

You also have to consider the sector or industry the company is in. To determine whether the dividend payout ratio is reasonable for the company, you'll need to compare it to other companies that are at a similar level of maturity in the same industry to get an idea. For example, it would make sense to compare Walgreens and CVS, but it wouldn't make nearly as much sense to compare Apple and Walgreens.

People often look at yield, but the dividend payout ratio may be more important. Yield gives a snapshot of return on investment (for the current share price). This measure, on the other hand, tells us what the company is actually doing with its cash flow.

Shares Outstanding

The number of shares outstanding is given by:

Shares outstanding = shares issued – shares in treasury

Shares in treasury or treasury stock are shares that the company keeps in its treasury. These are shares the company has bought back. Shares outstanding give us one way to get the amount of money paid per share:

$ Paid Per Share = (Net Income)/ (Shares Outstanding)

Dividend per Share

For many investors, this is the key piece of data they want to look at since it's the actual cash (if the company makes cash payments) that they are going to receive. Dividend per share is the amount of income from the company that you're going to get as a cash payment. The formula is just:

Dividend per share = (total dividend paid)/ (shares outstanding)

You can get the total dividend paid using the data in the previous section. Dividend per share is also given by:

Dividend per share = (Earnings per share)/(Dividend Payout Ratio)

If you are reading financial statements, unless you're investing in preferred stock, you'll want to look for dividends declared for common stock.

Top Reasons Companies Pay Dividends

Since companies have the option of paying dividends or not, it can be helpful to look at the reasons why companies would choose to pay them. We already have an idea of why companies would not pay dividends. Usually, new, growth-oriented companies don't pay dividends because they are reinvesting their money back into the company. That doesn't mean that strong, growth-oriented companies don't sometimes pay dividends. Apple, for example, pays dividends despite its near-record growth over the past decade or so. Of course, Apple had already been around a long time.

Paying dividends can be taken as a sign that a company is strong and confident about the future. If they are able to comfortably pay dividends and reinvest in growth, then that makes the company look solid. Paying dividends is also a mark of maturity. When a company has been around a long time and it's well established and mature, we usually expect that company to pay dividends. Of course, a mature company may not be aggressively pursuing growth.

What dividends indicate – given the company's ability to pay them, is that the company has a positive outlook about future earnings.

Dividends are also a good way to attract new investors to the company. While many investors are only seeking capital appreciation, there are a large proportion of investors that want to earn income off the dividends as well as enjoy the benefits of capital appreciation.

Note that if a company stops paying dividends or the dividend-price is reduced, this can have a negative impact on the share price. Elimination of dividends is definitely seen as a negative by investors. For that reason, if a company is going through a period of low profits or even losses, they may try to maintain their dividend payments if they have future expectations that they will turn things around.

An older company may want to reinvest earnings as well as new companies that are looking for aggressive growth. They may be interested in mergers and acquisitions (sometimes referred to as M & A), building new plants, entering new markets, developing new products, or investing in other new assets.

Investing in Preferred Stock

Investing in preferred stock is another way to get into income investing that is a little bit different than buying shares of common stock (when people talk about stock, they are usually referring to common stock). The dividend paid out to owners of common stock is dependent on the earnings of the company. Preferred stocks are also traded on a stock exchange. However, in some ways, they function like bonds. Preferred stocks have a fixed interest rate that is similar to the coupon rate of a bond. You can invest in preferred stocks directly, or you can invest in an ETF which invests in a large number of preferred stocks on behalf of investors in the fund. If you are interested in investing in order to receive income payments, preferred stock may be an option. They tend to pay higher yields, and preferred stock is generally liquid. However, it may be harder to sell preferred stock at your asking price than it is common stock. This will only be an issue if you are investing in single company preferred stock, if you invest in an ETF, the fund manager is handing buying and selling of shares that make up the fund, since an ETF works like a normal stock (its like a common stock in fact) buying and selling shares of a preferred stock is going to be a simple matter.

Preferred stock is becoming less common among most companies, except for the banking sector. Today, the vast majority of companies that offer preferred stock are banks. These companies include JP Morgan Chase, Bank of America, and Wells Fargo. If you don't mind investing in the banking sector, preferred stock may be an option to include in your portfolio. Dividend payments and yields for a preferred stock can be quite good, however. Bank of America, for example, at the time of writing, is offering a dividend of $72/share (annual) with a future yield of 5.59%. The preferred stock BAC.PL is $1,300 per share, however.

Trailing, Current, and Future Dividend Yield

Note that dividend yield may be quoted for different scenarios. Trailing dividend yield is based on the dividend paid over the prior period (usually the last year). The current dividend yield is given by:

Current dividend yield = (most recent full-year dividend)/ current share price

The future dividend yield is an estimate of the future yield. It uses current stock price and the dividend used is an annualized version of the first dividend paid for the year.

How much do I need to invest?

One question new dividend investors often have is they want to know how much they need to invest in order to make a certain level of dividend income. In most cases, you'll have to invest a pretty significant amount, and so, for a lot of people, the best strategy is to plan for building up a dividend investing portfolio over a long period of time. If you have access to several hundred thousand dollars of capital now, then you could start enjoying the income payments immediately. The amount that you need to invest is going to depend on yield, but like anything else in life, there are tradeoffs to be made. A company paying a high yield may have weaknesses that otherwise make the investment unattractive. Let's take a look at some specific examples to get an idea of what the market is really like.

The first thing you are going to want to do is set an income goal. So, let's say that you want to make $36,000 (before taxes) from your dividend income. Now, let's look at several ways that we could go about doing that. You can use a diversified portfolio, of course, and in chapter 4, we'll talk more specifically about setting up a dividend portfolio, so, in these examples, we'll look at some different examples of using one stock in order to reach our goal.

Let's start with a well-known heavyweight and suppose that you wanted to invest in Apple. Checking the stock ticker, Apple is currently trading at $175 per share. We'll use the quoted forward dividend from Yahoo Finance to make our estimate. It lists the forward dividend at $2.92, and the yield as 1.46%. Remember the dividend quoted is the annual payment. We'll first need to know how many shares we need, which is going to be the income we desire divided by the dividend paid per share. So, now its simple math, and we have:

Number of shares = $36,000/$2.92 = 12,329

To invest now and start getting the income, the amount we need to invest is:

Amount to invest = 12,329 x $175 = $2,157,575

That is a pretty hefty sum. If you have two million dollars that is sitting in the bank or invested in other stocks that don't pay dividends, that might be a good use for it. If you are a new investor just starting out, acquiring that much Apple stock is going to take you quite a bit of time unless you win the lottery. Whether it's going to be worth it or not is hard to say. It's difficult to predict what's going to be happening in five years in the tech sector, much less in 20 years.

What if you bought that Bank of America preferred stock we mentioned earlier? The forward annual dividend for that stock is $72, but of course, the share price is much higher. This time we only need:

Number of shares = $36,000/$72 = 500 shares

Amount to invest = 500 x $1,300 = $650,000

So, you see how yield and share price can be pretty influential. Some people reading this won't have access to $650,000 cash either, but more people will have access to that than they will two million dollars. Banking is probably not something that's going to go away, so it might be worthy of parking the $650k in the Bank of America preferred stock if you wanted to immediately generate that income.

The range of yields and share prices is quite dramatic, and there are many very low-priced stocks that offer high yields. Consider *Consolidated Communications Holdings*. Chances are, not many people reading this have even heard of it. This little stock trades on NASDAQ, and right now, it's trading for $4 a share (over the past 52 weeks, it did go up to $14 a share). The beauty of this one is the dividend yield of 38%. The annualized dividend payment is $1.55. So, let's look at how much we'd have to invest with this one in order to generate an annual income of $36,000.

Number of shares = $36,000/$1.55 = 23,226

That's a lot more shares than we'd need for either Apple or Bank of America, but this would only cost:

Amount to invest = 23,226 x $4 = $92,904

Now, we're getting into a range of investment that is more accessible to a lot more people. But you'd have to do research and find out who Consolidated Communications Holdings is and what their outlook is. Given the very low share price, it might not be that good (we leave it to you to do the research and find out). So, you'd have to ask yourself if you could afford to lose that $92,904.

Let's look at the Vanguard High Yield Dividend ETF. So, in this case, rather than buying stocks in individual companies, which can carry risk, we're investing in an exchange-traded fund. This is a fund that has invested in a large number of stocks that pay dividends, but rather than investing in the stocks themselves, we are buying shares of the fund. The dividends that are earned by the stocks in the fund are divided up and paid out to investors owning shares in the ETF in proportion to their ownership stake. The ticker for this fund is VYM.

Its dividend yield is 3.2% with an annualized dividend payment of $2.61. So we'd need:

Number of shares = $36,000/$2.61 = 13,793 shares

This is about Apple in terms of the number of shares. However, it's trading at $82. So we have:

Amount to invest = 13,793 x $82 = $1,131,026

This is a better investment than Apple. The reason is this ETF invests in 412 different companies. So, you get immediate diversified exposure, and you only have to invest $1.1 million instead of $2.1 million in order to realize the annual income of $36,000.

And over time, you have no idea what's going to happen to Apple. If it turns out that its best days are behind it, then you'd have to exit the stock, perhaps at a loss. When you invest in the Vanguard ETF, you're never facing this issue, since the fund manager is keeping up a solid portfolio that is highly diversified.

Example: How to Estimate Earnings

In this example, we're going to look up a stock ticker on Yahoo Finance and estimate the earnings from dividends per year that we'd make if we bought 500 shares. For our example, we're going to use IBM. It's a relatively older company that is still doing fairly well, so it's a good example of a mature company you might want to invest in if you were looking for a solid dividend stock. It's in the high tech sector, and although it's not anywhere near the heights it enjoyed in the 1980s when it was partnered with Microsoft, it would still be a solid addition to any portfolio. It's weathered many ups and downs both in its own fortunes and in the economy at large, and it's adapted to changing conditions by retooling its central mission.

Looking up IBM on Yahoo Finance, we find that it's trading at $127 per share. So, to buy 500 shares, it's going to cost us $127 x 500 = $63,500.

Yahoo Finance is a pretty useful website, especially because it's free. We can obtain financial reports for a company right there. Doing this for IBM, we can bring up the income statement. We actually don't need to look at these details, but let's do it just so you can see where things are located. You might want to refer back to our definitions earlier, but we immediately scroll down to find the net income and the net income applicable to common shares. IBM doesn't issue shares and so these are both the same:

Interest Expense	-723,000	-615,000	-630,000	-468,000
Income Before Tax	11,342,000	11,400,000	12,330,000	15,945,000
Income Tax Expense	2,619,000	5,642,000	449,000	2,581,000
Minority Interest	134,000	131,000	146,000	162,000
Net Income From Continuing Ops	8,723,000	5,758,000	11,881,000	13,364,000
Non-recurring Events				
Discontinued Operations	5,000	-5,000	-9,000	-174,000
Extraordinary Items	-	-	-	-
Effect Of Accounting Changes	-	-	-	-
Other Items	-	-	-	
Net Income				
Net Income	8,728,000	5,753,000	11,872,000	13,190,000
Preferred Stock And Other Adjustments	-	-	-	-
Net Income Applicable To Common Shares	8,728,000	5,753,000	11,872,000	13,190,000

Dates move from right to left, so 2018 is listed first at 8,728,000. Note that these numbers are in thousands, so the net income is $8.73 billion.

Next, we'll take a look at the balance sheet. Scroll down to Stockholder's equity. Here we find the retained earnings are 159,206,000 (again, in thousands) for 2018. For the previous year, we see the retained earnings were 153,126,000. So, the change in retained earnings was:

Change in retained earnings = 159,206,000 - 153,126,000 = 6,080,000

This is in thousands, so the change in retained earnings is $6.1 billion.

However, we really don't need to be going through the calculations. We can pull up the shares outstanding from the statistics tab, where we find that for IBM, the shares outstanding are 886.64 M.

Now, let's pull up the cash flow. The cash flow statement will tell us how much they actually paid in dividends in the past year. We are writing this book in the spring of 2019, so we'll use the data for the calendar year of 2018. Click on Financials, and then select Cash Flow.

Scrolling down, we find that in 2018, IBM paid 5,666,000 in dividends. Again, this is in thousands and so that is $5.67 billion. The dividend payment (annual) per share was:

Dividend per share = $5.67 B/ 886.64 M = $6.39 per share

The forward dividend, quoted on the Summary tab, is $6.28. That is an estimate but these are pretty close in value. But we'll use the real data, IBM's dividend payments seem to be relatively consistent.

So, if we bought 500 shares, we could expect to earn approximately:

$6.39 x 500 = $3,195

per year from the investment. Since dividends are paid out quarterly, we could expect to see a check from IBM in the amount of approximately $798 per quarter.

Special Dividends

A special dividend is a dividend payment that a company will make that is separate from its usual dividend payments. Sometimes, a company that doesn't pay dividends at all will make a special dividend payment. Companies may make a special dividend payment before a breakup or simply to get rid of some cash that it doesn't want sitting around. A special dividend is a one-time payment, and so, it's unlikely to impact the usual statistics you can look up about the company and their dividend payments. Depending on the fraction of the dividend payment, it can be subject to special or regular rules. Those subject to regular rules follow the rules that we outlined for dividends and payment dates discussed in the first chapter. A regular rule is followed when the special dividend is less than 25% of the share price. If it is 25% or more, then the special rules are followed. In this case, the payment is made and the following day is the ex-dividend date. If you sell the stock in this case and the sale falls after the record date but before the ex-dividend date, you will be paid the dividend but you must turn it over to the buyer of your shares when it's credited to your account. Option prices might be adjusted when there is a special dividend payment. Call option holders are not entitled to a special dividend.

Since a special dividend is a one-time event, it's not something that you should be thinking about when developing your overall dividend investment strategy. You can think of it as basically a random event, and it may or may not happen for any stock you own. But it will have no long-term impact.

Chapter 3

Important Investment Strategies

Some companies that pay high yields will allow you to reach the desired income goal without having to invest nearly as much money. But are they good investments? What criteria can we use so we don't foolishly park our money somewhere and end up losing it? The bottom line is you need to do your due diligence to make sure that the company sticks around for a significant amount of time and that it keeps paying good dividends. Also, if you need to sell your shares, you're going to be able doing so without taking too much of a hit. We'll also look at some different investment strategies you can employ to help improve the odds of success.

Are Bargains Worth It?

Some new investors might be tempted by stocks with low share prices that pay high dividend yields. Let's go back and look at Consolidated Communications Holdings. You'll recall that you could grab this stock at just $4 a share. The annualized payout for dividends is $1.55, which is comparable to many well-known companies. But who are these people, and is it safe to give them your money?

The first thing we'll note that is in the company's favor is they are trading on a major exchange, the NASDAQ. Being able to get listed on a major exchange is the minimal requirement that we could look for when doing due diligence.

First off, let's check out the company. It turns out this is a broadband company. From their website we find:

Consolidated Communications Holdings, Inc. (Nasdaq: CNSL) is a leading broadband and business communications provider serving consumers, businesses, and wireless and wireline carriers across rural and metro communities and a 23-state service area.

So, at least this appears to be a real business, and it's in a solid industry, apparently offering a focus on bringing broadband to rural areas. Looking at the history of the company, we find that it began trading on NASDAQ in 2005. Looking the company up on Wikipedia, we also find that they acquired a company called Fairfield communications, which allowed them to expand into 24 states. Since 2012, they've acquired four different companies.

It's hard to say whether that's good or bad right off the bat, they may be expanding too quickly for their own good by taking the easy way out by buying up similar companies. We are asking these questions because we'd like to get some understanding as to why the stock is only $4 a share. In fact, checking the history of the stock, we see that in late 2016, it was trading for $28 a share. Even at the beginning of 2019, it was around $11 a share, so we'd need to find out why it has dropped so much. In fact, we find that it plummeted all of a sudden in April. Looking at the quarterly financials, we see why – there was a net loss of $7.62 M in the first quarter, and more importantly, the year-over-year change in revenue was down 4.88%. However, this company still brought in $338 million in the first quarter, and lookup up their financial statements, we see that gross profit went from $421M in 2016 to $787M in 2018.

So, the company has some things going in its favor – and the price makes it look like a tempting buy. Let's summarize:

- The stock pays a really high yield.
- The dividend payment is fairly solid at $1.55 a share.
- The shares are dirt cheap, so we can acquire a lot of them and have an income stream right away.
- The company is in a good industry, broadband.
- From 2016-2018, gross revenue showed a solid and steady increase.
- Looking it up on Dividends.com, we find that it's been paying absolutely standard dividends. That is the same amount each quarter, at $0.3874 per share each quarter.

And here's a shocker. The company was founded in 1894! So, it's an older company, which offers us some assurance, given the very low stock price could indicate you'd be losing your equity soon if you put a bunch of money into this one.

Looking it up on Zacks.com (a good resource), we find that Zacks rates this stock a strong buy. It's also rated in the top 1% for its industry. Grades for value, growth, and momentum, are A, A, and B, respectively.

Checking Morningstar.com, the stock is rated *hold*. Not as encouraging, but they aren't advising investors to dump it.

So, it appears the disappointing quarterly earnings report made the share price crash. The next step you might want to invest your time in is learning about the company. What we need to know is what the company's plans are to improve its fortunes. In the news, we see that they've invested in a major project, expanding their fiber network in Des Moines, Iowa. That is probably a good start, but you'd need to read up on the company to make a decision. Remember, to earn $36,000 a year from this company, we'd have to invest roughly $91,000. So, it comes down to: are you willing to lose that money if things don't improve?

When investing, you can always put a stop loss order to sell your shares if things go south, so that you don't lose everything. On this company, we could put a stop loss of $3.50 a share, say. However, it's hard to imagine if this stock keeps losing the value that you will even be able to sell your shares. Remember that even though you're going to be doing your trades from a computer online or even on your smartphone, a real buyer has to be willing to pay your Asking Price for you to sell the shares. If this company is not turning its fortunes around, then there might not be anyone willing to take the shares off your hands at $3.5 a share – or at any price. This isn't like IBM, where if you needed to dump it, you could find a ready buyer.

There are other risks besides the stock price declining even more. If the company's fortunes don't improve, they may stop paying dividends altogether. In that case, you'd be stuck with worthless stock and it won't be paying dividends.

Of course, this is an older company, and it's been through a lot in the past century. There is a chance that they have a solid plan to turn things around, and part of your job as an investor is to read all of the publications the company puts out and any news articles you can find in order to determine this.

How to Evaluate Companies to Invest In

So, that was an introduction to finding a cheap stock and seeing whether or not it's worth it. Remember the old adage that you get what you pay for. In many cases, buying a solid stock, even though it's going to take either more money or more money and more time (that is, if you don't have the money to invest right now to generate the income you want), but it might be worth the extra effort. You can start slowly and build up over time.

The first thing to look for when evaluating a company is how its profits are trending over time. If you are a more cautious investor, then you're only going to want to select profitable companies, and probably only profitable companies who show steadily increasing profits. Those with a taste for some risk might be interested in companies like consolidated communications, that can be bought cheap, pays a dividend, and if the company gets profitable, the share price might rebound.

It's good to pick companies that are profitable, but better to pick companies that also show steady growth in their profits. As a part of your due diligence, you'll want to pay special attention to the cash flow reports for the company. Solid cash flow means money will also be flowing to dividends. Another reason to look at cash flow is we can get a handle on what the company is spending its money on, and what the trends are. Looking at Consolidated Communications, we see something interesting. Their capital expenditures increased significantly from 2016 through 2018. In 2016, (in thousands) the capital expenditure was 125,192. This increased to 181,185 in 2017 and was 244,816 in 2018. This might be one reason for the losses in the first quarter of 2019. The company has been putting a lot more effort into capital expenditures. This could be laying the groundwork for future profits; by helping them build out the infrastructure they need as a broadband company to acquire lots of new customers.

Let's have a look at some other companies.

This time, we'll take a look at a solid company called Abbvie, Inc. (ABBV). The current share price is about $75. According to Yahoo Finance, the forward dividend is relatively high, at $4.28, with a forward dividend yield of 5.39%. This looks like a very solid investment, unlike Consolidated Communications.

Looking at their financials, they have shown steady growth in their gross profit for the past 4 years. Looking at 2015, 2016, 2017, and 2018, we see gross profits of $18.6B, $19.8B, $21.5 B, and $25 B respectively. The company grew 16% from 2017 to 2018, which is about the upper limit you'll want to look for. Generally, you want to be aiming for companies that fall within a range of at least 5% annual growth up to about 15% annual growth. Companies that are growing much faster can create some issues with stock pricing if they fail to meet "expectations", and for dividend investing, we're also looking for companies that have their feet on the ground, so to speak, and so these would be companies that are growing steadily. AbbVie seems to fit this profile very well, and when you combine that with the high $4 dividend, this looks like an excellent investment. The share price is also reasonable. It's solid, but not too high. Let's check AbbVie to see how many shares we'd need right now for an annual income of $36k.

Number of shares = $36,000/$4 = 9,000 shares

Amount to invest = 9,000 x $75 = $675,000

For most people, that is still a hefty sum, but if you had that saved up in your retirement account, would it be worth moving it into an investment with this company? If you did, you'd be looking at getting a $36,000 payment every year rather than just having your money locked into a given stock. If you don't need the income right now, the $36k would be a nice bit of money to reinvest in AbbVie to increase your holdings each year or to invest in other stocks to diversify and grow your portfolio.

If you are just getting started with dividend investing, then AbbVie looks like it is a solid candidate to consider.

Let's look at some of the other metrics you'd want to consider when choosing a company to invest in. One of these is whether or not there has been growth in the dividend payment. To find out, pull up AbbVie on Yahoo Finance and go to the chart. Then, select the 5-year time frame.

Doing this, we find that recent dividends are ranging between $0.96 per share to $1.07 per share (per quarter). Looking back to 2017, we see that AbbVie was paying $0.64 cents per quarter, which is quite a bit lower but still a good dividend payment. This is a very good sign that the dividend payment has increased if you are a growth investor. Looking back to the beginning of the 5-year period, we see that at that time, AbbVie was paying around $0.49 cents per quarter. That is still a good value actually, for a benchmark comparison, remember that Apple at the time of writing is paying $2.61 annual.

Now, let's take a look at how the share price has changed over the 5-year period. At the beginning of the period, AbbVie was trading at $54 a share. Now, it's $75 a share, so the share price has shown appreciation. If you can find a stock with solid appreciation in the share price as well as in how much they are paying out in dividends, that's a great indicator of a solid growth company.

However, if you pull up the chart, you'll notice that in early 2018, it was trading for $123 a share. So, the stock price is quite a bit lower now, and it would be good to do some digging to find out the reason why this drop occurred. By October 2018, it had dropped to $80 a share, so it's been steadier since then so this isn't necessarily a catastrophic signal, but you'll have to put some more research into this to find out what scared investors away. Looking at the year-to-date chart, we find that the stock price has been fairly steady since the beginning of the year. By the time you are reading this, things may have changed in this regard. But so far, the company still looks like a good buy. But you have to be careful with a situation like this, you don't want to get in a bind where you want to get rid of the stock but doing so would leave you in a situation where you've lost a lot of the original capital you've invested. Let's say it dropped to $60 a share, and you decide you must sell because it's steadily dropping. At that point, you're looking at selling your 9,000 shares for 9,000 x $60 = $540,000. Remember that we purchased the shares for $675,000, so this amounts to a $135,000 loss, which is pretty substantial.

One way you can protect yourself from these types of situations is to use a stop-loss order. That is an order you place with your broker to sell the stock if the price gets below a specific value so that you can limit your losses. A stop-loss order is only executed if the share price matches or goes below the price you set in your order, otherwise, it's ignored. So, in this example, you could put a stop-loss order at say $70 a share.

That kind of technique is often used by day and swing traders to protect themselves from losing their shirts when they get themselves into speculation that went totally wrong. It's not entirely clear that is a good move with a stock like this, however, and you have very different goals if you're a dividend investor as compared to a swing or day trader. Remember that a stop-loss order is an automatic process. Since these shares are not just about momentary share price but also the income that they provide, you're going to be far more interested in the long-term prospects of the company. Placing a stop-loss order doesn't give you any room to think about your trades before executing them. That is good when you're a day trader, and you're trying to keep emotion from pushing you into a situation where you make bad decisions that can mean the loss of a large amount of money over a couple of hours, but when doing dividend investing, you're in it for the long haul, and so, you'll have to evaluate the long-term fortunes of the company and carefully consider them before making a move like that.

Another way to protect your investment is to buy a put option. This would give you the right to sell your shares at a fixed price, which is called the strike price. If you look at buying options, you'll find that there is a very wide range of strike prices, so you can set a level that you are comfortable with. But the advantage of this approach over stop-loss order is that it's an *option*. That means you are not required to sell the stock, ever. But you can sell it if you decide to. Let's see how this might work. Keep in mind that options contracts have an expiration date, so you'll need to look into that as well, and prices for the options increase the further out the expiration date is. The type of option you would buy in this case is a *put* option, which is something you'd exercise if the stock price crashed. In short, a put options contract is an insurance policy on your shares.

You could buy a put option with a strike price of $73 a share. The person that wrote the put options contract is *required* to buy the shares, and they have to pay the strike price, no matter what. So, in this example, if the share price dropped to $60 and the consensus was that it's going to keep dropping and this company is no longer a good investment, then it might be a good idea to sell at that point. But since you've purchased a put option, you can sell the shares for $73 a share even though the stock is trading at $60 a share. Ignoring for the moment fees and commissions, you'll get $657,000 from the sale.

But one other thing we need to look at is the cost of buying those put options. They are sold in lots of 100 shares per options contract. To protect your investment of 9,000 shares, you'll need to purchase 9,000/100 = 90 options contracts. So, let's find out how much these costs.

Looking up some options that expire in 3 weeks, a $73 put is priced at $0.94. That is a per share price, so you'd have to spend $94 to buy it. To get 90 options contracts, it would run $8,460. If we go out a full month, it's even more expensive at $1.19, or $119 per contract. That means you'd have to spend $10,700 a month to protect your investment, which is generating $3,000 a month. Obviously, this doesn't make much sense as a strategy.

So, you're better off using your judgment instead of relying on a stop-loss order. One advantage of a stop-loss order over a put option is that it doesn't cost anything. Buying "insurance" by purchasing put options can have significant costs, even though the cost is small relative to the amount of capital invested. Using put options might be reasonable if you are only trading stocks for their capital gains, as we saw in the example, they easily wipe out your dividend income.

One consideration to take into account with stop-loss orders is that stocks that are highly volatile might inadvertently trigger the stop-loss order. A highly volatile stock is one that has a price that fluctuates rapidly up and down over short time periods. So if a stock trading at $100 was highly volatile, over a trading day, it could drop to $96 a share, then up to $102 a share, and then back to $100 a share. If you were happy with $100 a share but had placed a stop-loss order at $96 a share, you would have seen your shares get sold even though you wanted to hold them as long as it was coming back to $100 a share (or higher).

So far, AbbVie looks like a fantastic buy for a dividend investor. Let's review the reasons why:

- It shows steady growth in gross profit, year to year. But it's not growing super rapidly.
- The share price is reasonable. It's priced where you would expect it to be for a solid company, but it's not too high. So, we aren't paying an arm and a leg for the shares, but its not some questionable stock like Consolidated Communications (which fits the definition of penny stock by the way, which has been modernized to $5 a share, but we consider also that it's trading on a major exchange).
- Dividends have been steadily growing. In fact, if you pull up the chart, dividends are higher now than they were when the share price was above $100.

Something else you'll want to look at is the fraction of net income that is paid out to dividends. Looking at dividends paid out by AbbVie over the past four years, we see they increased each year from $3.3B, $3.7B, $4.1B, to $5.6B in 2018. Net income in 2015 was $5.1B, so the percentage paid out in dividends in 2015 was 65%. In 2018, the percentage of net income paid out as dividends were 98.1%!

That may be an unhealthy situation. The company may not be investing enough capital back into their own operations and growth, and they may be using the high dividend payment as a strategy to attract investors in order to make up for other deficiencies.

Let's have a look at what this company does. The first thing we find is that it's a biopharmaceutical company. Revenue nearly $33 billion and 29,000 employees. That's a great sector with a lot of growth expected going forward, but you'll also notice that this company is a spin-off of Abbott Laboratories, a company founded in the 1880s- so mature and stable. So, we'll want to find out why Abbott decided to spin it off. Doing a bit of research, we find that Abbott wanted to split into two companies because they wanted to focus on medical devices, branded generic drugs, diagnostic assays, and nutritional supplements. AbbVie is actually the drug research arm of the original company and was the reason the company was founded in 1884. According to several articles, investors believed that Abbott was splitting the pharmaceutical part of the company off because that loss of an important patent for a drug called Humira was imminent. At the time, Humira accounted for half of the revenue.

Since this is a company built around the development of new pharmaceuticals, you'd want to know how much money they are investing in R & D. According to Statista.com, the company spent $3.3 billion in 2014, $4.3 billion in 2015 and 2016, $5 billion in 2017, and $10.3 billion in 2018.

From the perspective of wanting to see a pharmaceutical company developing new drugs that will come with patent protection, and hence, increasing the value of the company, it should be taken as a positive that they have ramped up their R & D spending. That increase in spending might be why the fraction of net income going to paying dividends has significantly increased, and this looks like a positive. The company is paying a solid dividend and is forward-looking in doing what they need to in order to drive long-term growth.

Looking at some of the news, there are some negative stories, and they may help explain recent declines in the share price. For example, we see that AbbVie sued the National Health Service in Britain, but the suit was dismissed in 2018.

Overall, I'd be comfortable making this investment and would be very pleased with the high dividend payment. It also looks like the company is willing to increase their dividend payments regularly and so is looking out for the interests of investors, and not just looking for rapid growth. You may have a different opinion and find that some of the negatives put you off when considering investing in this company, but we wanted to illustrate some of the things to look at when considering a dividend investment. Would I consider AbbVie over IBM and Apple? Yes and maybe. The reason is it's got more growth potential and it pays a high dividend. Apple's growth potential seems to have stalled, and its dividend is quite a bit less. In the case of IBM, it doesn't look to have much growth potential right now, but a $6 dividend payment is quite enticing. Probably a mix of AbbVie and IBM stock would be desirable.

Reinvesting Interest

One of the main principles used to grow wealth is to reinvest your earnings. This is the strategy that Warren Buffet used to grow such massive levels of wealth. Of course, he lives in the same house he's lived in for decades, and you might not want to grow large amounts of wealth for the sake of having it on paper. Most people go into dividend investing in order to get an income from the investment, in terms of cash that they can spend.

So, the first thing that you're going to want to look at is what your central goal is when it comes to dividend investing. Some of the different goals a person might be looking at include:

- Wanting a steady income ASAP. Maybe you already have significant capital you're willing to invest in dividend stocks, anywhere from $500k to $1-2 M or more.

- Growing your wealth over time. Maybe you're younger and want to build up as much net worth as possible for future dividend payments that could be used for income for early retirement, or even for a conventional retirement between ages 65-70.

- Maybe you're not looking for income from dividends at all, but you like the idea that they generate cash – money that you can use to invest in other assets. After all, you could invest in a company that doesn't pay dividends and hope for appreciation in the stock value, or you could find high-growth dividend stocks that also offer the opportunity for stock price appreciation, but at the same time, pay cash dividends, and then you can use the cash they generate to acquire more stock each year. This strategy can be very effective if you're having trouble raising cash to buy significant amounts of stock going forward.

Therefore, it's clear that what we do with the cash that the company's pay us each quarter is going to depend on why we are involved in dividend investing in the first place, and it's also going to depend on where you're at.

Let's revisit the concept of compound interest. This time, we'll consider a 20-year investment period, where we invest $650,000 in an investment that is paying a dividend with a 6% yield. We'll add a variance of 2 points, that is, the interest rate can fluctuate between 4-8%. We'll also suggest that we invest an additional $500 a month. What happens after 20 years? In this case, we used a calculator found on investment.gov. After 20 years, at 6% interest and contributing an additional $500 per month, you'll have $2,305,351.60. This is what we see when we plot the data:

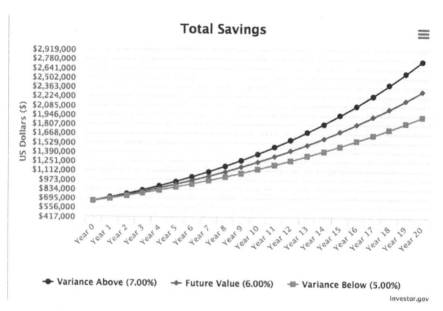

Even at 4% interest, you're looking at having grown your principal to around $1.8 million. That's pretty substantial. And that is the power of compound interest, especially when you add to your principal each month with new investments.

If you were buying AbbVie stock, for example, you could buy between 6-7 shares per month at the current share price, and so would substantially add to the number of shares with time. For the sake of simplicity, we'll say that conditions will stay about the same (of course, they won't over a 20-year time period, but this is just to give you an *idea* of how you could build your investment). So, we start with 9,000 shares that generate $36,000 in annual income, but we're putting that $36,000 back into the stock. That will give us an additional 480 shares per year at $75 a share. If we also put an additional $500 a month, we could buy another 75-80 shares per year. We'll say 78. That means each year; we add 558 more shares to our investment. After 20 years, we would have 11,160 more shares than we started out with. Our total number of shares would be 20,160. If it was still paying $4 a share, you would be looking at $80,640 in annual income 20 years from now, at which point, you could retire and simply live off the dividends.

Now, of course, these numbers are contrived. We haven't taken into account inflation or how much the dividend payment will change. Over a twenty-year period, there is a lot that can happen; the company could even go under. However, we doubt that would be the case for a pharmaceutical company that has been around since 1884, but then again, Bear Sterns, which appeared rock solid until the final months before its demise, no longer exists.

The calculator used above was a simple interest rate calculator. In fact, dividends can be more powerful than simply earning interest rates. You can find calculators that will estimate the value of your holdings at a future date and annual income from dividends, assuming that you're reinvesting the dividends. Of course, like the exercise we just did, they are suggestive but have limited value. They are basing their calculations on certain assumptions about the growth of the share price of the stock. Let's set one up at a useful website named dividendinvestor.com. Here, again, we'll assume we start with 9,000 shares, a stock price of $75 a share, starting yield of 6%, and 20 years to hold the investment. AbbVie shows solid growth in dividend payments, so we'll assume a 2% growth rate. Using this calculator, we find that after 20 years, our initial $675,000 holding has grown to $2,899,214.58. That is some substantial growth! The annual income increased from $36,000 to $41,000 in the first 12 months, but after 20 years, it's increased to $242,508. That could be a pretty high income, but again, these are rough estimates, and we don't know what will happen to inflation and so forth in the meantime. Remember that the U.S. government has amassed a huge debt, which could eventually cause major problems in the economy if it's not dealt with at some point between now and then.

Nonetheless, you need to take these lessons to heart. You can get a lot of growth from a solid dividend investment over time, and reinvesting the proceeds until you want to retire is a vital part of your strategy if maximum growth is one of your goals. When you do that and add to your investment by continuously buying more shares, you can end up with a very nice nest egg.

Of course, we note that some people might need the money right now, and that's why they are considering investing in a dividend stock. You can still benefit in that case, over time, the dividend payment may continue to grow, but if the company eventually stagnates, that may become an issue. You can also adopt a strategy of taking some of the cash and reinvesting a portion of the cash. For example, if you're bringing in $3,000 a month, maybe taking $2,500 out as cash and reinvesting $500 a month is something that would work out for you.

Another consideration is the time that you're planning to hold the investment and use it to generate income. If you are only going to have it for 5 years or even 10 years, maybe reinvesting in it isn't a good idea and your needs for the immediate cash are more important.

Many of the issues that arise from investing in a single stock can be mitigated by diversification or possibly even better by investing in dividend ETFs. That way, you aren't subject to having your outcomes determined by the fate of a single company and can invest to assure future growth no matter what happens.

If you are not planning on retiring soon and have an adequate income from other sources, you should reinvest your dividend payments by purchasing more shares of stock.

Dollar Cost Averaging

Dollar cost averaging is an investment strategy that seeks to average out the volatility that comes with changing stock prices. So, if you are looking to invest in a stock that is currently priced at $75, it might go down to $70 at times, and it might rise to $80 at others. The same holds true for an index fund. If you have a fund that tracks the S&P 500, there are going to be lots of ups and downs over the short term. A jobs report or bad GDP growth report can cause the value to drop substantially. On the other hand, if the GDP growth report is better than expected, share prices might rise.

Your goal, in general, is to buy low and sell high, as they say, but it's hard to know when you are really buying low. It's a guesstimate as to when the bottom will be reached when stock prices are declining.

What dollar cost averaging does is it removes the guessing game by purchasing shares of stock at regular intervals no matter what the share price happens to be at that moment. At times, you are going to be paying a higher price for the stock. So using our example, if the short-term (meaning over a year or so) price of Abbvie fluctuated between $70 and $80, sometimes, you'd be buying at $80, but at others, you'd be buying at $70. So, the prices that you'd be paying for your shares would be evening out (averaging) with time. This is a set-it and forget-it strategy and you won't have to sit there paying attention and agonizing over the share price. You just set a rule; say buy $500 worth of shares on the 10th of each month, and stick to it, knowing that, over time, the fluctuations in the price you're seeing are going to average out to the overall trend in the stock price (which of course may be rising). The more purchase dates you set, the better this process will work. Purchasing once a month might be a crude estimation, so you could break up your purchases into once a week, buying 1 or 2 shares every Friday instead of buying 6 shares one time per month, for example.

If you choose to adopt dollar cost averaging as one of your investment strategies, you need to be disciplined and stick to it. If you haven't used it before, you might have a lump in your throat when you are purchasing shares at a higher price, worrying that the stock price might drop and you feel like you're missing out on a good deal that may happen. But it may not and none of us can tell the future. That is why dollar cost averaging is a good technique to have in your investment toolbox.

Diversification

Any long-term investor should have a diversified portfolio. One of the problems with stock market investing is that people can get overcome by emotion that can cloud their judgment. It can happen no matter what kind of investor you are. For day traders, they can panic when a stock starts dropping fast leading them to sell before they should, or they might get greedy if they see it rising, and end up holding onto their stocks too long.

But you need to realize that emotional issues clouding judgment when it comes to stock market investing are not something that is limited to day traders by any means. Many times, long-term investors can get rattled by market ups and downs and make many bad decisions as a result. If you are a long-term investor, then you should ignore the fluctuations in the market, including recessions. Remember that recessions are temporary. For some reason, people tend to have a viewpoint that when a recession comes and stock prices drop that their wealth tied up in stocks was "wiped out". People will even say this after a recession ends and stock prices are rising again. In the vast majority of cases, the wealth represented by the asset value of your stock holdings is going to recover and do it relatively quickly after a recession bottoms out.

The important thing about recessions and even run of the mill bear markets is that, in reality, these are buying opportunities. You shouldn't be holding out for a bear market, however, it might be a while before one shows up on your doorstep. But if you are using dollar cost averaging, at the very least, you should continue using your regular purchase schedule as stocks are declining. In fact, if you have the available capital, you should actually increase your level of stock purchasing during a downturn.

Here's the rub, when there is a downturn, nobody knows how far it will go. Day traders and other speculators might be looking for supposed "signals" in the data that indicate a turning mood among investors, telling them that a buying frenzy is about to erupt. This isn't to say the tools used in technical analysis of stock trends are not useful, they are, but you should take them with a little grain of salt. It's very easy to get misled by a short-term increase in buying or selling, and while people try to mitigate that possibility by relying on multiple tools, the reality is that's a very difficult problem to overcome and nobody can be sure they are right about what's going to happen next. In a mathematical sense, while human behavior can be predicted a large fraction of the time – think about how often it completely and utterly surprises you.

That same unpredictability is operating in the stock market too, remember that, ultimately, it's the people that are behind decisions to buy or sell a stock. So, in the end, nobody knows when there is going to be a genuine market shift or not. But by using dollar cost averaging (and accelerating your purchases until prices start rising again), you can help take some of your emotion out of it and keep making purchases when the stock is a good buy.

Another problem with stock market investing is when people fall in love with a particular product or company. This happens all the time, and humans seem to be primed to fall victim to this malady. Many times, people develop an infatuation toward a given company. Apple is one historical example of this, where people have become so slavishly devoted to the company that it can do virtually anything and they will be lining up with their credit cards out to buy whatever product the company spits out. Now, over much of the time, this was fairly justified. Apple was cranking out game-changing products ever since the iPod was developed. However, even after Steve Jobs passed away and the company began a slide into the world of the mundane with only incremental changes, the devotion of many "fanbois" continued where Apple was concerned.

Becoming infatuated with a company often has a rational basis, but it can also be something that is extremely destructive. The recent controversy around medical device maker Theranos is a case in point. If you get right down to it, the bottom line for

Theranos is that the company is/was a complete fraud. That isn't to say everyone who worked at the company was a fraud, but the CEO was definitely a fraud. Even when this was crystal clear, many investors had become infatuated with the CEO (Elizabeth Holmes) - who was a very intelligent young blonde woman who tried to emulate the Steve Jobs vibe by wearing black turtle neck sweaters and dropping out of school. Unfortunately, being very intelligent isn't a guarantee that someone isn't mentally ill, a con-artist, or who knows what. It's possible that things simply got out of control. Holmes came up with some ideas for medical testing devices, and this got the attention of several heavyweight backers. Soon enough, the devices were being tested and used by large companies like Walgreens. But it was gradually revealed that the devices didn't work as claimed. It may be the case that Holmes started out with good intentions but got pressured to fake it when there was so much weight on her shoulders and huge pressure to produce a winner, and it was becoming known to her that it wasn't going to work. Or she may have been a fraud from the very beginning, we may never know. However, she has been charged with massive fraud by the Securities and Exchange Commission, so more information about this may be forthcoming.

In the case of Theranos, it's pretty clear that investors and large backers – who included political heavyweights Henry Kissinger, George Schultz, and billionaire and Secretary of Education Betsy DeVos – were so infatuated that they let their judgment get completely clouded. None of them have indicated why they were so taken by the company and its founder, but if you read some of the original patents filed by the company, the fraud should have been obvious from the beginning. They sounded like "Star Trek" inventions, and the burden of proof for accepting they could work should have been very high. This is definitely a case where due diligence should have played a central role in any decision-making, even in the case of Walgreens that partnered very early with Theranos, probably seeing dollar signs as people would be going to Walgreens for many medical tests as opposed to laboratories that their doctors send to them now. But instead, people were easily taken by Holmes and the claims the company was making.

Theranos is an extreme example, but many investors get smitten with a wide range of companies and believe that the company is the next "sure thing". Unfortunately, it's a lot easier to see a "sure thing" when looking back on it. For example, Amazon was certainly a good bet to make in the late 1990s. But who would have really known how things would have turned out? At that time, Amazon was competing with quite mature and well-established companies like Borders Books and Barnes & Noble, not too mention a nationwide network of independent and small book stores that drove a huge fraction of traffic when it came to selling books. Nobody could have possibly foreseen that Borders would soon completely collapse and those small bookstores throughout the country would be nearly completely wiped out. Also, nobody would have been able to imagine that Barnes & Noble would be too slow to respond and be inadequate with their response. They are still around but are a shadow of what they once were.

Another thing that few people could have imagined was that Amazon would be extremely aggressive in their drive to expand into other areas, not only completely taking retail but getting into areas like cloud computing. That said, wouldn't it have been great if you had bought a few thousand shares of Amazon in 1998 and just held onto them?

By the way – Amazon doesn't pay dividends. Maybe they will at some point in the future, but given the incredible drive Bezos has, he is now looking at going into space, it's hard to imagine the company becoming a dividend investment any time soon.

So, we can come to the central lesson of this section. Let's pull all this together. The first point is we shouldn't be the type that panics, letting short-term losses that will pass in a year or two govern our decisions about holding stock. There are times that you'll want to sell a stock, but that would be when a company was failing, not just because there is a temporary economic slowdown.

The second lesson is that you should never let infatuation with one company, or a product that it makes, govern your investment decisions or the role that they play in your portfolio. Yes, it can't hurt to invest in some companies that you are excited about that have potentially disruptive products. However, you'll need to recognize that many times, your "bets" are going to end up dead wrong. Sometimes, they will be right, of course, but ahead of time, it can be quite difficult knowing which is which.

This brings us to the lesson of diversification. Any long-term investor should be using a diversification strategy and not putting all their eggs in one basket. At the very least, your fate should not be tied to a single company. If you had put all your investment capital into Theranos, you'd be broke today. If you had put it into Apple, you might be a millionaire. There were reasons in 2007 or 2008 to put a lot of money into Apple, but Theranos obviously made a persuasive case as well. When it comes to investments, letting everything ride on one company is a serious misallocation of your judgment and your money.

So, what does diversification mean, really? At a minimum, you should be investing in 10 different companies. That is probably the lowest level of diversification that should be considered.

However, you should not invest in more than 15-20 companies. The reason is that you should be devoting a lot of energy to your due diligence. This means studying the markets, knowing what the economy is doing, when the Fed is going to increase or decrease interest rates and what that might mean for each of your investments. It also means following politics, decisions by politicians might have implications for your stock holdings.

All those things apply whether you have one stock in your portfolio or whether it's 100. However, you also need to keep a very close eye on each company you invest in. You need to be aware of who the management team is. What are their backgrounds and how have they performed in the past? You need to be aware of the company making important changes to the management team.

You'll also need to study the company. When it was founded, what industry it's in, how it's performing, and what its future plans are. Is it heavily invested in R & D? Hoping to enter foreign markets? Taking steps to address problems? These are all important issues that should be addressed if you are going to be putting your life savings behind a company.

If you are doing this research properly, then it is unlikely you're going to have time to closely track more than 20 companies effectively. So, if you are planning on investing in individual companies, plan on choosing 15-20 companies.

Diversification doesn't end there, however. You should also be looking at investing in multiple industries or sectors. Something might happen that could hit one sector but not others. For example, at the time I am writing this, many politicians are jumping on the regulate-the-tech-sector bandwagon. This can have major implications for tech companies that collect data, like Facebook, Google, and Amazon. Depending on how far our brilliant politicians go, the impact could be devastating.

Even so, this may not impact other sectors like banking, agriculture, or healthcare.

So, you will want to look at all the major sectors you can invest in, and allocate some of your investment capital in different sectors. That way, if one sector gets hit particularly hard if the others don't, then your overall investment portfolio will remain viable.

Diversification can also be taken in other directions. Another way that you can diversify is to invest in companies that are based in other countries. You may want to invest in Japanese, Canadian, European, and Chinese companies. Or you might want to target some investments to emerging markets like Brazil. There are many issues that can come up with this, so a great deal of care is required. Take your amount of due diligence and triple it.

Normally, financial advisors also urge people to allocate their investments in different ways depending on age and also investment goals. So, the older you get, the more you should put your money into safer investments, which for them, involves putting money into bonds, money market funds, and maybe safe instruments like bank CDs. As a dividend investor, you can also follow that procedure but you may also be avoiding it since dividend investing is a relatively safe way to invest that provides an income (something you'd be looking for if you were investing in bonds, say).

Now, within the world of dividend investing, there are many options you can use to diversify your portfolio that goes well beyond simply choosing a wide variety of companies to invest in across different sectors. For example, you can invest in exchange-traded funds, something we will discuss in the next chapter. Or you can invest in REITs. There are many ways to stay completely focused on dividend investing while pursuing multiple paths. So, for example, you could build up a portfolio that was allocated in such a way that 50% of your capital went to individual companies that you selected, 25% was in REITs and MLPs, and 25% went to exchange-traded funds.

The possibilities are nearly endless. Some investors might be using investments in dividend companies as a part of a larger, overall strategy. So, you could combine dividend investing with an aggressive growth strategy to drive more capital accumulation.

The point is diversification doesn't just mean investing in 10, 20, or 30 different companies. There are many ways to diversify your investments, but the fundamental truth behind all of them is that you're looking for a way to mitigate risk.

Since we are a big believer in taking advantage of downturns as investment possibilities, the risk that you're trying to mitigate is that you don't want to have one company take you down with them. In 2007, it would have been a really bad deal if you had put everything into Bear Sterns. While we can argue that if you were closely following the situation, a sell signal was flashing red, who could have really blamed you for investing in it? Before it started crashing, it was trading at $170 a share. It had been founded in

1923 and survived the Great Depression. It could have been seen as a good investment.

Rebalancing

Rebalancing is a process of buying and selling shares once a year to get your portfolio back to a place where you are satisfying your long-term investment goals. Each year, it's inevitable that some stocks are going to increase more than others, and by the end of the year, the amount of capital invested in each company isn't going to match what you had planned for your long-term future.

For simplicity, let's say that you have 25% in banking sector companies, 25% in retail, 25% in healthcare, and 25% in high tech companies. At the end of the year, you might find that the shares in the high tech companies significantly outperformed the others, so you might end up with a portfolio with a capital allocation where there is 30% in banking, 15% in retail, 15% in healthcare, and 40% in high tech. If you decide at the end of the year that you are committed to sticking to your original plan, then you're going to sell 5% of your investment in banking sector companies and 15% of your investment in technology sector companies, and then reinvest in the sectors that dropped in proportion. So, you'd buy shares in retail and healthcare until all your investment sectors had 25% each.

Selling off the shares and buying new ones in this manner helps you "rebalance" your portfolio. It will also help you book profits by selling shares that were in the sectors that saw growth, you take your profits and reinvest them.

This is an important strategy if your asset allocation has been designed to help you reach certain goals, such as value, growth, or income.

Another way you can look at using rebalancing, when we are specifically considering dividend investing, is to put more of your money into companies that pay higher dividends. After all, the goal for dividend investors is to have shares that pay back a return beyond simple stock appreciation. So, if you have a company that pays smaller dividends but whose shares significantly increase in price over a year, you can sell those shares and take the profits, and then invest those profits into a company that is paying a good dividend.

Let's say that your portfolio consisted of just three stocks. Apple, IBM, and AbbvVie. Remember that the dividends paid by these companies are about $2.61, $6, and $4, respectively. Suppose that you have 1,000 shares of each, but then Apple shocks everyone by releasing a new phone, and their share price jumps by a large amount. Even then, although the dividend might increase, it's probably unlikely to reach the level that IBM is at, and even AbbVie. So, you could sell a fraction of your Apple shares, and then use the profits to buy more shares in IBM and AbbVie.

DRIPS

If you haven't heard of DRIPS before, as a dividend investor, you should learn what they are and determine whether or not you're going to want to use them if they are available for the stocks you invest in. A DRIP is a *Dividend Re-Investment Plan.* A DRIP will automatically take your cash dividends and buy new shares of the stock with the proceeds. It may also allow you to buy fractional shares so that all of your money is invested. DRIPS may come with a fee, but many leading companies that pay dividends offer no-fee DRIPS. These companies include AbbVie, Exxon, Johnson & Johnson, and Aflec among others.

If you are in your investment plan for the long haul and aren't looking to take cash out right now, using DRIPs can be a way to enforce discipline. If you receive the cash payments, you might be tempted to spend it. In this case, signing up for a DRIP plan will ensure that the money goes straight back into the purchase of new shares. Reinvesting is a key component of growing the size of your portfolio over time.

However, DRIPs aren't for everyone. If you are planning to use your investments to take cash out now, that is, you're doing this for immediate income, then you're not going to want to use a dividend reinvestment plan. The reason is your dividends will be reinvested into the stock automatically. So, you wouldn't receive any cash payments from that stock.

Another person that might not want to use DRIPS is someone who wants to reinvest the money from their dividends, but they might be planning on investing that money into other stocks. If you sign up for a dividend reinvestment plan, you are giving control over the dividends to the company, which will automatically buy more shares in their company on your behalf. If you want to invest elsewhere, then don't use a DRIP, and instead, take the cash payments, and then you can reinvest it as you see fit.

If you don't use a DRIP, you also have the advantage of splitting up the money, you might want to take some in cash either to spend or to invest elsewhere, but reinvest part of your dividend money in the company. If you retain control over your investments and don't sign up for one of these plans, then you'll be able to do what you want to do with the money.

Dividend reinvestment plans can definitely work for you if you are at a point in your life where you don't yet want to take the cash out from the dividends. A DRIP will help you enforce discipline, and it will enable you to automatically take advantage of the compound interest nature of reinvesting your dividends back into the stock and growing your assets in the process. It will also help build time into the equation since time + interest = huge money.

Consider that each time you buy a new share of stock, you will begin earning money off that new share the next time there is a dividend payment. Keeping things as simple as possible, suppose we had one share of stock in a company that paid $10 a share in dividends and it's trading at $10 a share. The first time we get a payment, we get $10. You could take the $10 and go out and buy a pizza!

Or instead, you could use the $10 to buy another share of stock. Now, you have two shares, so the next time there is a dividend payment, you get $20. What to do at this point? Well, you're facing the same conundrum, and maybe, you'll buy two pizzas. Or you could reinvest with $20, having purchased the extra share of stock last time around means that you can buy two shares this time.

So, now you're up to four shares of stock. Another dividend payment comes and you get $40, and you can buy four more shares of stock, doubling your total investment holdings.

You can see where this is going.

It's possible to have a DRIP with your brokerage or directly with the company. Typically, there aren't fees associated with the transaction, but if you invest directly with the company, they may offer some discounts on your stock purchases. In other words, you may be able to get some shares at prices that are lower than the current trading price of the stock.

Before we leave the topic of DRIPS, let's go over the arguments against them. We've already discussed the first argument, and that is the income argument. If you are in dividend stocks because you need the income now, then a DRIP is not going to be something that would work out for you.

A second reason to consider avoiding DRIPS is that if you are using rebalancing in your portfolio, the automatic reinvestment of the DRIP might cut into your plans. Each quarter, you're going to automatically own more shares of any stock that is part of a dividend reinvestment plan. Growing shares in those particular stocks may not align with your overall investment goals. Also, it makes it harder to purchase shares from other companies, since the cash you could have taken out will be automatically reinvested.

Another reason that you might not want to have a DRIP is that when dividends are paid, it's going to buy shares on your behalf automatically. So, you'll be forced to buy shares no matter what, even if the price isn't favorable. You might be at a market peak, and if you have a DRIP, well, that's life. Of course, if you are using dollar cost averaging, that will mitigate this to a degree. Remember that dividends are typically paid on a quarterly basis, and so, you'll have dividend reinvestment purchases of shares that will happen four different times a year. And they will more than likely be able to take advantage of different pricing for the shares.

The bottom line with DRIPs is if you are early in your investment life, and you've begun putting money in a solid dividend stock, then having a DRIP makes sense. The fact that your proceeds are going to be automatically reinvested will make sure that your own personal foibles and emotions are not getting in the way of strict market discipline. You can always turn a DRIP off at a later date.

There are also other ways to rebalance your portfolio as well, so that excuse might not be good enough when it comes to deciding that you are going to avoid having a DRIP.

On the other hand, if immediate income is your goal, then a DRIP is probably not something you'll want to pursue.

When to Sell Dividend Stocks

There are many reasons that you might find yourself in a position where you want to sell a dividend stock. But before we get into those specifics, we want to make sure that you remember the ex-dividend date and its importance. If you sell the stock before the ex-dividend date, even if it's the day before, then you will lose out on the dividend payment. Whoever owns the stock on or before the ex-dividend date is the person who gets the payment. So, if you decide to sell a dividend stock unless there is a compelling reason you should hold off until the ex-dividend date has passed. That way, you will get the last dividend payment associated with your stock ownership.

Something else to note about selling dividend stocks is that when the ex-dividend date goes by, it's typical that the share price is going to drop by the amount of the dividend. This is because, in the eyes of investors who are looking to buy shares in the company, the shares have lost a little value (the amount they would have gotten from the dividend). Imagine that a stock is trading at $100 and it pays a dividend of $2 a share. People looking to buy the stock before the ex-dividend date may have many reasons to buy the stock, but one of them is definitely getting that $2 per share payment. Once the payment is made, and they have to wait another quarter, then the stock isn't worth quite as much and so it drops by the $2 they missed out on, and will now be at $98 a share. Over time, it's going to regain that lost value, but don't be under the illusion that you can pocket the $2 dividend letting the ex-dividend date pass and then simply sell the stock for the original share price of $100.

Of course, there is a risk that the share price is going to lose value for other reasons if you hold the stock too long.

There can be many reasons to sell your shares. For one, you might need to rebalance your portfolio. So, you'll want to sell off some shares if the current holding has grown out of proportion to where you want it to be.

Another reason to sell a dividend stock is maybe you've found a stock that pays a better dividend. The stock market is always dynamic if it's anything, and so there is always the possibility that while you thought your original stock was very attractive, you find later that there is another stock that pays a higher dividend and the company has solid fundamentals.

The reliability of a dividend payment is an important consideration as well. First off, is the dividend payment growing with time, or at least staying the same? Hopefully, it's growing. You're going to want your dividend income to beat inflation. Also, a growing dividend is a part of the indication that the company is growing, and with more net income, they are happy to share more money with investors. On the other hand, if the dividend isn't reliable, it's growing smaller, for example, or changing erratically, that is a bad sign for a dividend investor. In that case, you might want to bail on the stock before things get worse.

That's one reason that AbbVie is so attractive, they've steadily paid dividends and the size of the dividend steadily increases. They even increased their dividends when the stock price had dropped.

Something else you'll need to keep a close eye on is the financial health of the company. You will also want to keep an eye on its bond rating, even if you aren't buying bonds from them. If their bond rating drops, the company may be late or missing payments – an indicator of trouble. Look at the cash flow of the company and read all the financial statements. If the company is showing signs of deterioration or trouble ahead, by less cash flow, then you're probably going to be better off opening yourself up to finding a better, more solid investment.

A company that starts taking on large amounts of debt might be in trouble as well. Of course, there are legitimate reasons for a company to take on debt. So, you might see your dividend payments shrinking as the company gets bogged down in making interest payments on its debt, or simply has a problem managing money in general.

Crashing stock prices paired with higher yields can be a problem as well. That is something you'll see with Consolidated Communications. They may be focused on keeping their historical dividend payment despite a load of financial problems elsewhere. Why would they do that? Because keeping the dividend payment at the same level - even though the share price is deteriorating – will help them attract investors. The lesson here is to always do your analysis. If a company's dividend payment is rising, find out what the reason is. If you find out that it's rising in order to keep the yield at a certain value, that could be a trick that's being utilized to pull people in, and you'll want to stay away.

Besides taking on a large amount of debt or a crash in the share price, another thing to look at is the stock buybacks. If a company can't buy back stock or has significantly backed off from stock buybacks, this might be a clue that they are going to be heading for trouble. They may not have enough cash on hand to meet obligations, and so, their ability to pay dividends may be compromised.

These factors indicate that investing blindly is not an option. Remember, you need to be looking at the company's financial statements so you have a clear idea of where they have been and where they are going, you need to read the company's website and any publications so that you know what their big plans are to stay profitable or regain profitability, and you need to be ready to cut ties when it becomes clear that a company is no longer a good investment.

Bear Market Opportunity

As we said earlier, when there is a bear market, let the fools follow the lemmings over a cliff. Crashing stock prices are an opportunity to pick up a lot of shares at discount prices. If there is one thing that can be guaranteed, a bear market is going to be followed by a rise in prices. Even the Great Depression began seeing large increases in stock value from 1933 onwards.

For example, let's have a look at Bank of America stock over the period of April 2007 through April 2010. The stock dropped from $50.90 with a dividend payment of $0.56 a share in April 2007 to a share price of $3.14 a share on March 2, 2009. If you had bought 1,000 shares in April 2007, it would have cost you about $50,000. But if you had bought 1,000 shares in March of 2009, it would only have cost you around $3,140. And incidentally, that dividend payment had dropped to a penny a share in March of 2009. Today, the stock is trading at $27 a share, with a forward dividend of $0.15 per quarter. That isn't a good dividend and I wouldn't recommend buying the stock for the dividend, but if you had bought the shares at $3.14, you could sell them now for $27,000 and have made a profit of nearly $24,000. As we discussed earlier, Bank of America could be an investment to consider if you bought the preferred stock. Of course, it is expensive on a per share basis.

The point is, recessions and bear markets are buying opportunities. Look at another stock, this time Johnson and Johnson. It dropped from $71 a share to $48 a share. Throughout the entire economic crisis, the dividend payments for Johnson and Johnson remained relatively constant and even raised a bit from $0.41 a share to $0.46 a share. That is a good sign of a solid company that can weather storms. Of course, Johnson & Johnson makes many things that people need for their day-to-day lives, and the 2008 recession being a banking crisis (in part anyway), it would have been more attractive at the time than Bank of America.

You should do your research now so that you are well prepared for the next bear market. Look for stocks that did not slash their dividend payments during the recession. That is a good sign of a stock you might want to be in over the long term. Remember, they always come, and no matter how prepared we are, the economy has its ups and downs. But rather than fear it, imagine how much better off you'll be if you start seeing bear markets as investment opportunities.

Dividend Aristocrats

A dividend aristocrat is a company that routinely raises its dividend payment. In fact, Standard & Poor maintains a listing of the top 50 companies called the dividend aristocrats. According to their specific criteria, a dividend aristocrat is a company that has raised its dividend at least one time per year over the past 25 years.

You can look up the list to see who these companies are and you could invest in each of these companies or pick a list of 20 of your favorites out of this list to make your own dividend aristocrats list. However, buying individual stocks yourself in this manner could be problematic. Companies move on and off the list all the time, especially during major economic downturns. Prior to the 2008 financial crash, many banks were on the list, and at the time, they were considered among the most solid investments around. But we all know what happened, and so, simply investing in companies on the list might have gotten you into some trouble.

While some companies were forced off the list, many held their dividend payments steady right through the crisis and even increased them. You can study the data yourself and find some of these companies; they may or may not be a consideration for investment. Some of them actually pay a low rate per share but have higher yields.

The best way to invest in a group of companies like this is to find an exchange-traded fund that will do it for you. Unlike mutual funds, exchange-traded funds have minimal fees, and as we noted earlier, they trade just like stocks. One fund to consider is SDY which invests in many of these companies. SDY is yield weighted, and so gives more weight to companies that pay higher yields making them a larger proportionate share of the funds' investments. With a fund like this, the funds managers will decide what companies to invest in or sell, so you won't have to worry about it. As we mentioned earlier, it's trading at about $95 a share and paying $2.12 a share on an annual basis (it's actually paid out quarterly). The ETF has investments in AbbVie, A T & T, IBM, Cardinal Health, and Verizon Wireless, among other companies.

There are other good dividends ETFs available, however. One you should consider is the iShares Dow Jones Select Dividend Index Fund. The annualized dividend payment is $3.48 with a 3.67% yield. This ETF is trading at $94 a share. So, it's slightly less per share than SDY, but pays $3.48 per share as opposed to SDY paying $2.12 a share. If you can make more money for a slightly smaller investment, that sounds worth considering. The goal of the fund is the same. It's looking for stocks with consistently growing dividends. Some of the holdings of this fund include Microsoft, Apple, JP Morgan Chase, Johnson & Johnson, Coca-Cola, Verizon, and Chevron. Of course, it also includes AbbVie.

Chapter 4

High Yield Investments

In this chapter, we are going to look at some of the more unconventional ways you can invest in dividends, the high yield investments. We have touched on these a little bit in the first chapters, these include real estate trusts or REITs, master limited partnerships or MLPs, and BDCs. Each of these has their advantage and disadvantage, so let's have a look at them and see whether or not they are something that you might want to include in your investments.

REITS

A REIT is a real estate investment trust. There are two types of REITs. The most common type is an equity REIT, which invests in properties. It makes money by collecting rent and selling properties. The second type is called a mortgage REIT, and it makes loans, earning profits from the interest paid with the loan. When dividend investors buy shares in a REIT the vast majority of the time, they are going to invest in an equity REIT.

Equity REIT is typically going to hold commercial properties, but they can hold multi-family properties as well. You can invest in REITs of different types, for example, one might invest in office buildings while another may hold retail or industrial properties.

A REIT makes getting into real estate investing rather easy. They trade like stocks and are relatively inexpensive. Look for share prices around $100 a share.

A good example of this is Digital Realty Trust (stock ticker DLR). Looking this up on Yahoo Finance, we see that (at the time of writing), it's trading at $115 a share. The forward dividend yield is a healthy 3.67%, and the dividend is $4.32, which is a very attractive payment. This is an attractive REIT to invest in because it's a digital data center REIT. So, they own facilities that are used for cloud computing. There is no doubt that this will be in demand in the coming years.

Welltower is a healthcare-oriented REIT, investing in everything from hospitals to old-age homes (stock ticker WELL). The share price is $82, and it has a yield of 4.67% and a dividend payment of $3.48 per share.

If you are noticing, REITs have pretty healthy dividend payments. You might be better off investing in DLR than Apple if your goal is a higher level of income. DLR costs less per share, so the barrier to entry is lower and yet it pays around $2 above what Apple is paying for the dividend.

REITs exist for virtually every type of property. Consider Gladstone (LAND), which buys up and rents out farmland. AMH (American Homes 4 Rent) is a REIT that invests in single-family homes which it rents out. It's trading at $24 a share. That one does have a low yield and dividend (0.83% and $0.26, respectively), so you might want to hold off on that one for now, but we mention it to illustrate that there are a wide variety of choices when investing in REITs. Other REITs even own such obscure things as cellphone towers.

If there is one thing virtually everyone has discussed investing in at one time or another, it's probably real estate. However, if you were to invest in real estate, you have to get loans or spend a large amount of money. Let's compare investing in a REIT to buying a house and renting it out.

First, let's look at renting a house. Suppose you bought a home for $250,000, say in Denver, Colorado or Salt Lake City. We want to pick a midsized to large Western city to avoid getting caught up in worrying about out of control sky-high rents in places like San Francisco, Los Angeles, or New York City. The best case scenario is you pay cash. A home in that price range might rent for around $1,400 a month. On top of this, there are property taxes, but we'll assume that the tenant covers the over expenses. Taking property taxes and any incidental expenses into account, which in western cities that aren't super crowded aren't too high; let's say that you profit $1,100 per month. At that price, it would take you 228 months to make the $250k back. That's 19 years. Basically, during that time, you make zero profit.

If you put $25,000 down and took out a loan for the rest, a 15-year mortgage would cost you around $1,655 a month. That might not cut it in your market, so you could eat the difference in what rent was being paid, or you could opt for a conventional 30-year mortgage. In that case, with 3.92% interest, your mortgage payment would be $1,092. So basically, you're breaking even, but the tenant is paying the mortgage.

If you invest $250,000 in DLR instead, you're going to get dividend payments of around $8,700 a year. While the $250,000 is locked into the investment, there is no mortgage. If you wanted to, you can reinvest the money from dividends and buy an additional 75 or more shares per year and take advantage of compound interest to grow your principal over time.

At this point, it might be a matter of taste which you prefer, but what REITs allow you to do is get in properties without the hassle of having to actually own properties. You can invest in actual real estate by buying a few houses if you have the cash or the credit. But you're going to be dealing with tenants, having to pay for the upkeep of the properties, periodically having to remodel the homes or at least putting in new flooring and updating bathrooms. It's not as simple as it looks from the outside. With REIT investments, you can get into diversified types of real estate while other people handle all the hassles, and getting out of it is as simple as putting in a sell order with your broker.

REITs are entities that don't pay corporate taxes, and they distribute most of their earnings to the shareholders. Typically, they pay out 90% of their earnings. Before buying into a REIT, you're going to want to look under the hood just like you would before investing in a company. What you're going to want to know is how their income is being generated. With REITs, you're going to look for Fund from Operations which is also listed as FFO. The types of things that go into calculating FFO include net income, depreciation, interest income, and gains or losses from selling properties. REITs will also have an adjusted FFO, which adjusts the FFO by taking into account some other items that are subtracted from the FFO calculation. These can include money spent on maintenance of the properties, rent, and unrealized gains.

Some REITs might calculate their FFO differently than others, but you can use the ratio of Share price to FFO. The higher the value, the better.

As with stocks, you're going to want to look at the performance over time, and in particular, their cash flow. You will also look at yield and dividend payment to see if that is something which will fit into the ranges of dividend payments that you are willing to accept. If the FFO has a solid growth rate over several years, it's a good REIT to invest in.

Like every other kind of investment these days, you can use an exchange-traded fund to invest in REITs. This has several advantages. The first is diversity in the types of exposure. That is, instead of buying one REIT yourself that is focused on one type of property, you can invest in an ETF that is invested in dozens or hundreds of REITs. They are also going to be invested in many different types of REITs, so you can get exposure to hospitals, land, digital, home rentals, and so on.

IYR is a real estate REIT ETF provided by iShares. It invests in companies that are on the Dow Jones Real Estate Investment Index. Another famous and well-regarded REIT ETF is Vanguard VNQ. You can get on the websites to see how these have performed. According to iShares, if you had invested $10,000 in IYR 20 years ago, today, you'd have $50,000 in equity. Of course, this doesn't take into account the money made (and possibly reinvested) from dividends.

REITs can be an interesting investment to add to your portfolio, but be aware that they do carry some risks. The biggest risk is interest rate risk. Being in real estate, REITs may be taking out a lot of loans. Higher interest rates may mean higher expenses for the REIT, but there are other factors you will have to take into consideration, such as the context of the higher interest rates and what's happening in the economy at large. Depending on circumstances, higher interest rates may mean more competition for properties (especially commercial properties) that could mean higher profits for the REIT. In any case, a REIT should be taken to be a long-term investment, so the usual buy-and-hold strategy applies here unless you have compelling reasons to put your money elsewhere.

MLP

Now, we turn our attention to MLPs, which are master limited partnerships. As we noted in the introductory chapter, this is a business which is a partnership that is traded publicly like a stock. MLPs trade on major exchanges. However, it acts as a partnership, so profits will be taxed when investors receive the distributions. An MLP is required to distribute the cash it has on hand to investors. It has general partners and limited partners, as an investor, you will be a limited partner. You are not involved in any way in the day-to-day operations of an MLP.

The law requires that an MLP has to pass 90% of its income to investors. Congress restricted MLPs to certain sectors because they are upset that MLPs don't pay corporate income taxes but are publicly traded. As a result, MLPs are limited to real estate, energy, and finance. Since most real estate operations are REITs, the vast majority of MLPs are in the energy sector. Oil and gas operations are something you'll find in MLPs. Usually, this is in transportation or infrastructure company so it will transport oil, own refinement facilities, or oil pipelines. They are not as sensitive to oil and gas prices as a direct energy company like Exxon, because they are paid by the volume of oil or gas they can transport.

An MLP is a tax-advantaged to the investor, which means you can offset your tax bill quite a bit. Depreciation and depletion are actually passed along to you, as the investor and you handle that on your own taxes, which can result in very substantial tax savings. This happens because as a partner, you have a stake in the assets of the company so can take advantage of the depreciation. Note that if you invest in an MLP ETF, you don't get these tax advantages.

Although you should probably not get involved in investing in an MLP ETF, it's easy to invest in MLPs because they trade like regular stocks on major exchanges. However, they are bought and sold in "units" rather than shares. They act like dividend stocks, but the income paid from MLPs is called a distribution rather than a dividend, and it's paid quarterly. Income from distributions is treated as a return on capital for tax purposes. This means that the majority of your distributions from the MLP are not taxed until you sell your shares (units). You could avoid the tax by simply not selling; otherwise, you can sell them and pay capital gains taxes. Yields from MLPs tend to be very attractive.

For example, Enterprise Product Partners (EPD), which owns oil pipelines, offers a yield of 6.11% with a distribution of $1.75 (paid quarterly, annual amount). The price per unit (aka price per share) is about $25. Magellan midstream partners (MMP) is trading at $62, with a yield of 6.54% and a distribution of $4.02. Incidentally, "midstream" is energy jargon for a company that transports energy. "Upstream" would be the actual drillers.

Since the tax advantages are lost if you buy into an MLP ETF, you're better off investing in the MLPs themselves. One thing we can be sure of is that energy isn't going anywhere anytime soon, even if Alexandria Ocasio Cortez thinks it's going to be completely transformed in 12 years. You can bet that she is wrong about that and these are good investments.

You'll want to investigate the financials for any MLP you consider investing in. There are three items of interest. The first is the amount of cash distributed by the MLP to the partners (investors). Second, you should know the DCF which is given by DCF (Distributable Cash Flow). This is basically the cash left over after expenses and paying the general partner. This will include net income, depreciation, and capital expenses like maintenance of the pipelines or building new ones, etc.

Once you know DCF, you'll also want to know the coverage ratio or CR, which is DCF divided by the cash distributed to the unit holders. What this tells us is how healthy the MLP is as far as being able to make the cash distributions to unit holders. If the coverage ratio is less than 1.0, that means the MLP wasn't able to make its payments to the shareholders. So, probably one you'll want to avoid. Before investing, check the coverage ratio.

Since you aren't going to be using an ETF because of the tax implications, if you want to invest in MLPs, you should handle your own diversification. You should invest in about 5-10 MLPs. Pick MLPs with high yields and coverage ratios that are above 1.0.

BDCs

A BDC is an investment company. The formal name is Business Development Company, and it generally invests in small to mid-sized businesses. Business Development Companies typically target young companies that are in need of capital in order to grow. These are typically companies that can't obtain funding elsewhere.

Congress set up the BDC as a structure in 1980. If the company meets certain requirements as set by law, such as paying out the minimum required amount of cash flow to investors, it can be structured as a BDC and avoid paying corporate income taxes. So, a BDC essentially acts as a pass-through company. Many of them pass as much as 98% of their income to investors, which can result in very high yields.

In practice, BDCs can act like venture capital firms, investing cash for equity into small and medium-sized businesses that are growing. At other times, a BDC will provide loans to businesses. Sometimes, the BDC acts as a salvage operation, investing in or lending money to a business that is in distress, for the purpose of turning its fortunes around.

Typical yields for BDCs range between 8-12%.

An example of a BDC which provides investment capital to help distressed companies turn around is Saratoga Investment Corporation (ticker SAR). Investments can be up to $20 million.

Many BDCs offer secured loans to small and medium-sized businesses. An example BDC that does this is Apollo Investment Corp (AINV). A company like this is considered a solid investment. Since it's giving out loans, it earns a steady stream of income in the form of the interest payments.

Chapter 5

Using Options for Income

Dividends aren't the only way to earn money off the shares of stock you own. You can also earn money writing options contracts if you're not averse to the higher level of risk. In truth, the risk is relatively low and you can derive a solid income from selling options contracts. What's more, you could combine options with your other means of investing to increase your income potential. For example, you could invest in a stock that paid a solid dividend and reinvests the dividends as time goes on. But you could still make cash from the shares by writing covered call options on them. However, you have to be aware that there is a risk you would have to sell the shares. The real risk is relatively low for two reasons, however. The first is that few call options are actually exercised, and the second is that even if you're forced to sell your shares, you will still probably make a profit and can reinvest the proceeds from the sale in another stock.

What is a call option

A call option is an option to buy shares of stock at a fixed price. We call the fixed price the strike price. An option comes with an expiration date, and there is a wide range of expiration dates, but typically, they are going to expire in the near term like 3 weeks or a month. Underlying any options contract are shares of stock, and there are 100 shares of stock for each options contract.

Options contracts trade on exchanges that are set up specifically just for them, so there is an entire world of options traders living off the stock market. This works to your advantage. The reason is that most options traders are interested in profiting off the trading of the options contracts themselves, but they aren't really that interested in owning the shares of stock. But be aware that some people who buy options contracts are interested in buying the shares, so you may end up having to sell your shares in some circumstances. However, the data shows this doesn't happen most of the time, and so as we'll see, this provides an opportunity to earn a monthly income from your shares.

Pricing of Options

First, you should familiarize yourself with some options in the marketplace so that you know how they are priced and you can get an idea of how much money you can make off your shares. To write an options contract, you will need to own at least 100 shares of the underlying stock. The price of the option is going to vary on two things; it will vary on the price of the underlying stock itself, but remember that the option also has an expiration date. So, the price of the option is also going to be impacted by the expiration date. The closer you get to the expiration date, the lower the price of the option – all other things being equal. A few days out from the expiration date, the price of the option is no longer impacted by the time left until the option expires. We call the decline in price from the time until the option expires time decay, and the value that goes into the option from the amount of time left on the contract is called the extrinsic value.

The value of the option that comes from the underlying stock is called the intrinsic value. Ideally, the intrinsic value would come directly from the price of the underlying shares. Remember, there are 100 shares for an option contract, so a rise in the price of the underlying share price by $1 would mean a $100 rise in the price of the option. Similarly, a $1 drop in the share price would mean a drop in the price of the option by $100.

In the real world, the relationship isn't that cut and dry, but there is a number that you can look at in stock data that will give you a good estimate of how the price of the option will change with changes in the underlying share price. This is a Greek symbol called delta. It's a number that ranges between 0.0 and 1.0, so if Delta is 1.0, then the change in the price of the option will be ideal that is a $1 rise in share price will result in a $100 rise in the price of the option. If Delta was 0.7, then the price of the option would rise to $70 for every $1 rise in the price of the stock.

The idea of a call option is to give a bullish investor, that is someone who is expecting the stock price of some investment to rise in the near term, the ability to buy shares of stock at a cheaper price that is agreed upon beforehand. So say that you own 100 shares of a stock that is trading at $100. Maybe a bullish investor out there believes that the stock price is going to rise to $105 a share. But they want a bargain and they're only willing to pay $102 a share. So, they can buy a call option with that strike price. If at any time that the call option hasn't expired, the share price goes above $102 a share, that would mean that the buyer of the option could exercise their rights to buy the shares. And the seller of the shares would be obligated to sell them at the discounted price of $102.

Now, let's look at it from the seller's perspective. You may be bullish on the stock over the long term, but you may not believe it will pass $102 a share. Also, chances are you bought the stock back in the past for a lower price than it's currently trading at. Therefore, if you had to sell the shares at $102, you wouldn't be too bothered, since you would probably be making a profit anyway – even though that profit might be quite a bit lower than the profit that you would have made selling them at $105 a share. However, as we'll see in a second, some of that difference is going to be covered by the money you get by selling the option.

An option isn't free. Someone that wants one has to buy it. Prices are quoted on a per share basis. So, if you look up options prices, you will need to multiply the quoted price by 100 to get the price someone would actually have to pay. Let's look at our favorite dividend stock, Abbvie.

The share price at this instant is $75.70. There are call options with strikes above and below this share price. For a call option, when the market price of the share goes above the strike price for the call option, the price of the option goes up by a lot. Options with prices above the current share price are still worth money (until they expire), but the higher you go in strike price above the current market price, the lower the cost of the option.

So, we see a call option expiring in three weeks that has a strike price of $76.50, or $0.80 above the share price. It's estimated that there is a 69.7% chance of profit, meaning that before the option expires, the share price has a 69.7% chance of being lower than the strike price of $76.50. The price is quoted as $1.40.

So, if you owned 100 shares of Abbvie, you could sell this option for $1.40. Since the contract covers 100 shares, you can sell a contract on 100 shares for $1.40 x 100 = $140. If you own 1,000 shares, you can, therefore, sell ten contracts and earn $1,140. The payment for an options contract is called the premium. So, the premium is money you earn off the stock, and odds are you will be able to take the money as profit and still keep your shares. But be aware there is a risk that if the stock price went up to $77 a share, which would put your price below the market price, you might have to sell your shares for $76.50.

You can reduce your risk by picking a call option with an even higher strike price, making it less likely that you'll have to sell your shares because the probability of the stock price reaching the strike price and exceeding it gets smaller with each higher strike price you consider. Remember, options expire, with most of them expiring in the near term. That means it's likely the three or four weeks will pass and you'll still have your shares. Especially with a stock like Abbvie that isn't all that volatile.

So, let's suppose that the price did go to $77 and you had to sell your shares for $76.50. In fact, let's suppose it goes to $78.50 so that you would lose out on $2 a share. First of all, note that you probably aren't losing anything, what you are losing is potential profits. If you had purchased the shares in the past, say in June of 2017, you paid $67 a share for them. So, even though you can't sell them for $78.50, you're still selling them at a higher price than you paid for the shares. Plus the money earned from selling the options contract is yours to keep. So, you've made $1.40 per share from that, and so, you're nearly at the $78.50 price when you add all that up.

In the jargon of options traders, a call option is in the money if the market price of the stock goes above the strike price of the options contract.

If you are buying and selling shares looking for capital gains, then this scenario isn't going to bother you at all. However, if you are a dividend investor, you do have that risk staring at you that you will lose the shares and so be out the dividend.

But the fact is most options traders are looking to make profits buying and selling the options contracts themselves. Therefore, they are probably going to end up selling an options contract to someone else if the option goes in the money. Why would they do that rather than buying the shares? Because an options contract that is in the money is worth more, and so they can sell it and take their profits.

Let's look at some prices of the money call options for AbbVie that expire on the same day. A $75 call is priced at $2.21, so it would sell for $221. A $73 call is priced at $3.58, so it would sell for $358. That would mean if you had 1,000 shares, you could sell 10 options contracts for $3,580. That isn't a bad passive monthly income.

Dividend Stocks aren't volatile

One of the good things about dividend stocks when it comes to this strategy is they don't tend to be volatile. A volatile stock that has wild price swings is more likely to exceed the strike price, which might cause you to have to sell your shares. Since most dividend stocks are slow and steady as they go, growing but doing so at a slower and steadier clip as opposed to say, Tesla, Netflix, and Amazon, you're less likely to face the prospect of having to sell your shares.

However, the risk that you will have to do so is real, and sometimes, it will happen. So, be sure to pick a strike price that you are willing to live with, so if you are not comfortable selling the shares at $76.50, pick $77 or whatever suits you. Just remember the higher the strike price the less money you're going to earn.

The further out you go, the more money you make

Calls that expire months in the future can be sold for high premiums. Looking out six months for AbbVie, we see that a $77.50 call sells for $4.73 per share, so 100 shares per option mean we could sell one option contract for $473. If we owned 1,000 shares, then we could sell 10 contracts for $4,730.

You can go even further out in time. If an option expires more than nine months into the future, it's considered a LEAP. That stands for Long term Equity Anticipation Security. For AbbVie, we can check a year and a half into the future and see that a $70 call is selling for $11.28, so the price of the options contract is 100 x $11.28 = $1,128. Just remember that the longer you have until option expiration, the more chance there is that someone might "call" the option and force you to sell your shares. So, you should choose a strike price that would be above the price you paid for the shares when you bought them.

Put Options

We can use put options to mitigate the risk of having to sell our shares with the covered call option, but first, let's get a little bit of familiarity with what put options are. A put option gives the buyer the option to buy shares of stock at a particular price. Like a call option, that price is called the strike price. One way that options traders use this to make money is they buy a put option for a stock that they think is going to go way down. Then, if the stock does go down, they buy 100 shares at the cheap market price, and then they exercise the option and sell them to the writer of the contract at the strike price. The profit is the difference between the strike price and the market price. Let's use an example.

Suppose that a stock is trading at $100 a share. You buy a put option with a strike price of $90 a share, but you don't own the stock. But you're basically shorting it; you would do this if you think the stock is in for a massive decline. Suppose that the option sold for $2, which would be a total price of $200.

Suppose that the stock does decline significantly before the expiration date of the option. For the sake of illustration, imagine that it drops to $40 a share. So you buy 100 shares for $40 x 100 = $4,000.

But since you own a put option with a $90 strike price, you can exercise it. That means you can sell the shares for $90 a share. So you make $90 x 100 = $9,000. Your profit is $5,000 from the sale of the shares. You also had to pay a premium for the put option, which was $200. So your total profit is $4,800.

Of course, the numbers are a bit absurd, but they were chosen to illustrate the point and show you how to put options work and why people might buy them.

Earlier in the book, we described how you could use a put option as a kind of insurance on your stock (in theory anyway).

Expiring Worthless

Now, if time runs out on the option and the strike price isn't in a favorable position, that means that the option expires worthless. For a call option, if the market price is below the strike price, the option is worthless at expiration. That's because nobody would want to pay more per share (the strike price) than they could pay on the open market. So, they are not going to exercise the option under any circumstances.

For a put option, if the share price is above the strike price at expiration, then the option expires worthless. That's because the person who would exercise the option would be forced to sell them to you at a lower price than they could get in the market, and that doesn't make sense.

Selling in the money call options

So, we see one way that someone might profit from a decline in stock price, but there is a way you can profit from a decline in stock price using covered calls as well. This is done by selling a call that is already in the money. So, let's say that for the sake of argument, there is going to be bad news coming out in 3 weeks about AbbVie. Anticipating that the stock price will drop, and so make a call option that is out of the money worthless, you write a call option but one that is in the money now, so you can charge a higher premium. So, if the current market price is $75.70, you can sell a call option for $74 if you expect the share price to drop below that. The price for that option is $2.85 x 100 shares = $285. Again, if you had 1,000 shares, that means you could make $2850. If the share price doesn't end up dropping, you might be forced to sell your shares, so choose a share price that you are comfortable with. If it does drop below the strike price, then you keep your shares and made $2,850 from the sale of the option premium.

Summary

Selling call options is another strategy you can use to increase the amount of money that you earn from your shares. The risk is that the option will be exercised. More often than not, the options are not exercised. Remember that the options contracts have value in and of themselves, and so most of the time, they aren't exercised because options traders are looking to profit off the short-term trading of the options contracts. Also, many options traders are looking for ROI off the smaller investments that options require. While it might cost a trader $221 to buy a call option with a $75 strike price for AppVie, it would cost them $7,500 to buy 100 shares of stock at that price. In many cases, the investor isn't interested in laying out the money to buy the shares and we have an order of magnitude difference between the price of the option and the price of the shares.

While this strategy can be attractive, the risk factor of having to sell the shares will put off many dividend investors. But it might work for you.

Chapter 6

Top 10 Mistakes Made By

Dividend Investors

Dividend investing tends to attract more level headed people. However, as a beginner, you're likely to make mistakes along the way. By learning what the top mistakes beginning investors are likely to make ahead of time, you can avoid getting into too much trouble, and maybe avoid getting into trouble altogether. In many cases, the problem with the stock market is not so much that people don't have a magic wand that lets them pick the best possible stocks, but instead, it might be people routinely make mistakes that get them into trouble. Avoid making the mistakes and let the general uptrend of the stock market take care of everything else.

Getting anxious to receive a dividend

The way this works out is you see a stock with a good dividend payment, and so, you try and buy it as close as possible to the ex-dividend date to get paid right away. Doing this is creating a situation where you can get yourself into trouble by letting emotion start to take over. Normally, emotion isn't as much of a problem for dividend investors, but once it gets its foot in the door, you can start running into financial problems. The key to avoiding this problem is to take a long-term investing viewpoint and buy shares on a fixed and regular basis.

Only paying attention to yield

It's true that yield can be an important indicator, but you shouldn't be entirely focused on it. Remember that if you are investing in dividends, it's the dividend payment that is the most important metric. Going back to Abbvie (yet again), the forward dividend is $4.28 per share, with a yield of 5.39%. Now, remember the BDC we mentioned a couple of chapters back, Apollo Investment Corp? That BDC had an incredible yield. Checking it today, the yield is 11.52%. But the dividend is only $1.80.

Let me ask you, would you rather make $4.28 per share from AbbVie or only make $1.80 per share? That $4.28 is an extra $2.48 in your pocket, per share. So an investment in AbbVie might be more prudent if making money from the dividend income is your goal.

Another reason to not get too hyped up by yields is they can be inflated by a declining stock price. One of the first companies we looked at was Consolidated Communications, which has a shockingly high yield of 38%. And guess why? Because their $1.55 dividend payment is for a stock that is only selling for around $4 a share. A high yield on something that has, unfortunately, become a penny stock may not be something that fits your investment goals.

Whether or not yield is important will depend on a wide variety of factors that you are using to evaluate potential investments. But don't just focus on yield alone, look at the entire picture.

Failing to look for growth

On average, dividend investors tend to be more conservative than other types of players in the stock market. Maybe not as conservative as people who will only buy mutual funds, but certainly more conservative than your average growth investor. The goal with dividends is to seek out stable companies that are mature, but you should also get growth-oriented companies that are paying dividends into your portfolio as well. While they may be paying a lower dividend right now, over time, a growth-oriented company may end up paying a higher dividend than an old stalwart like Wells Fargo or Johnson & Johnson. You will want to look at the company's history of paying dividends and see if you spot a trend, and that trend would be increasing dividend payments. Don't look at absolute amounts, look at percentages, and choose companies that raise their dividends by a significant percentage at least once a year.

Not investing in dividend ETFs

Individual stocks are fun to invest in, and people love the excitement of doing the research and being able to track all the different companies. That's great and you can get some great buys in your portfolio. However, you should also invest some of your money into ETFs so that you can take advantage of the massive diversification. This will also act as a hedge to help keep a part of your portfolio stable and secure. I would recommend putting between 25-40% of your dividend investments into 2-3 different ETFs, probably one that tracks dividend aristocrats, and also include a REIT to diversify your exposure.

Not Diversifying Enough

We've covered a wide range of investments in this book, and you should be investing in all of them. How you allocate your investments are up to you, but strictly buying stocks might be leaving opportunities on the table. For example, there is no reason not to invest in REITs, either individually or through an ETF. You should also invest in at least five MLPs so that you can take advantage of the high distributions and enjoy the tax advantages as well.

Only investing in stocks

Well, okay, we are repeating ourselves … but there are other good investment possibilities out there for income investors. We included one in this book, that was the possibility of selling covered call options. You can use that to generate income now or to magnify the impact of compound interest by reinvesting the money you get from premiums. Another investment that people oriented toward dividends should consider is investing in bonds, which can help generate more monthly income. It's not as lucrative as it once was, due to the lower interest rates we've had over the past 20 years, but it can still add to your income and provide some level of protection for your money. ETFs are a great way to invest in bonds and diversify beyond just investing in dividend stocks.

Buying stocks because they are cheap

Remember that sometimes you get what you pay for. That doesn't mean you have to buy the most expensive stocks on the market in order to build wealth using dividend investing but remember, some stocks might have a low price – because they are not a good investment. As we've noted before, a declining stock might try to use a high dividend payment or yield in order to try and attract investors, who otherwise aren't all that thrilled about investing in the company.

Now, sometimes, a company that is set for better days in the future might have a low share price. Remember, to figure out where the company stands, you need to look at the company's fundamentals. Look to see how things are changing over time and research the company to see what new products are coming out and so forth. Sometimes, a cheap stock really is a bargain, but you can't go on price alone.

Being Afraid to let go

One of the downsides of dividend investors who by nature are going to be more conservative is that they sometimes can't let go of a stock that isn't worth holding anymore. It can feel like you're betraying your plans when you are investing with the hope of generating a lifelong passive income from dividend payments, and the stock starts performing so badly, it's clear to the mind but not the heart, that you need to get out. Use the same muscles in your brain that you would use to evaluate a cheap stock you were thinking of buying and analyze the company. Read what the experts are saying about the company. A good rule of thumb is to use three stock services to see what they are saying, so you could use Zacks and Morningstar plus one other as we discussed in parts of this book. If 2 out of 3 agree that something is a sell or a strong sell, then sell your shares and move on. You can use the proceeds from the sale to invest in a new stock or put it into an existing stock already in your portfolio that is already performing better.

Not taking your taxes into account

Remember, investing in the stock market isn't free, and any cash you take out is going to be taxed. You may not like it but that's the way things go. So, it's important to be familiar with the tax laws that apply to dividend stocks so you have an idea of what you're going to have to pay from the various profits you are making in this enterprise. You don't have to have the expertise of an accountant, but don't take money out and say you're going to worry about the taxes later. Have some idea of what the taxes might be and be sure to pay estimated taxes so that you don't find yourself falling behind later and then having a massive tax bill. Another concern and this is the one I was really getting to when it comes to failing to take into account taxes, is that you overestimate your profits. When you figure taxes into your transactions, you might find out that your gains are not as great as you thought they were. If you are going to be building an income from dividends, it's a good idea to have an accountant rather than trying to fly alone using tax software.

Not Doing Due Diligence

The final mistake that we'll look at in our list is taking a cavalier attitude toward your investments. Many people don't put the time into studying the market and the companies they are investing in or want to invest in, and as a result, they don't invest nearly as well as they could. Rather than keeping abreast of what's going on, they just invest in what they feel like investing in. That could make the difference between making $26,000 a year or $75,000 a year from your investments. When you are going to buy a stock, you should be able to clearly explain to someone else the exact reasons that you would buy the stock and what you're expecting to get out of it, as far as both the dividend payments and capital appreciation of the shares.

Chapter 7

Tax Implications

This part of the book is the least enjoyable. But let's face it; most of us don't know much of anything about how our complex tax code is going to be applied when it comes to the stock market and to dividends. If you're a beginning investor, that is definitely true. The first advice that should be given is that if you build up a large portfolio of stocks, you're going to need to use a professional accountant. But having some understanding of the general rules will help as well. Remember in the last chapter, one thing we mentioned is you don't want to get into a situation where taxes end up cutting into your profits.

Ordinary versus Qualified Dividends

The first thing to be aware of is the difference between ordinary and qualified dividends. The kinds of dividends that we've been talking about in this book are ordinary dividends. That means that the income from them is, well, ordinary. In other words, the proceeds are taxed as ordinary income.

A qualified dividend comes from a capital gain. Following the kind of investments that we have described in this book, you're probably not going to be getting qualified dividends.

Example: Suppose you're in the top tax bracket. You get $100,000 in qualified dividends. That is taxed at the capital gains rate, so you'd owe $20,000 in tax.

Example: You get $100,000 in ordinary dividend payments from your investment in IBM. Since they are more than $1,500, you have to fill out a schedule B and then report them with your 1040.

Tax Forms

The dividends that you get from an investment in dividend stock will be reported on a form 1099-DIV. If you are getting dividend payments from an s-corporation or trust, they will be reported on a form K-1. Note that investments in vehicles like an MLP will generate a K-1.

Dividends that you reinvest

Unfortunately, the geniuses in Congress didn't see that it was fit to prevent this in the interest of promoting investment, but dividends that you reinvest are still subject to tax, so you have to report any dividends that you receive on your tax return and pay taxes for ordinary income on them.

Example: You earned $25,000 in dividends, but you reinvested them buying more shares. You still have to pay the tax on them. Like the example above, they are more than $1,500, and so, you need to report them on schedule B of your 1040.

Some tricks to lower your tax burden

If you have an individual retirement account, your money in the account is allowed to grow tax-free. One downside is that the wise old men of Congress limit how much you can invest in an individual retirement account to around $5,500 -6,500 per year depending on age. However, there is a nice trick you can use with dividends inside the individual retirement account. You can use the account to buy dividend earning stocks. Then, when the dividends are paid, they are paid inside your IRA. That means that they are tax-free, and you can reinvest them inside the IRA. Keep in mind that when the money is taken out of your IRA after you retire, if you have a traditional IRA, you're going to have to pay taxes on it at that time (a Roth IRA means you pay taxes on the money now, but the money is tax-free later when you withdraw it).

So, the procedure to avoid paying taxes on dividends is:

- Open an IRA or use an employer retirement account like a 401k
- Buy dividend stocks inside the retirement account
- Reinvest the dividends inside the retirement account
- That way you won't face taxes on the dividends

The same trick can be used to massively grow your retirement accounts using covered calls. So, you buy shares inside the IRA, and then sell covered calls with the IRA account. Odds are good that most of the time the options aren't going to be exercised. So, you make, say, $2,500 profit a month selling covered calls, and it's inside your IRA, and it's going to be tax-free since the account is allowed to grow tax-free. Then you use the funds from your covered calls to keep buying more shares. So, although you're only limited to putting in a relatively small amount each year after you've built up a few hundred shares, you can start earning money from selling covered calls and reinvesting the dividends. Then, when you start pulling money out of the IRA when you've retired, you will pay taxes on the money at that time.

Chapter 8

Starting Late

In this chapter, I would like to briefly address a problem that far too many Americans have today, despite the opportunities all around us for investing. The fact of the matter is many people have failed to save and invest and now find themselves 50 and older without any net worth. Millions of Americans can't even come up with the cash to pay a $500 emergency. This situation means that tens of millions may be heading toward retirement without any investments to speak of or only a small 401k that was provided by their employer. They are hoping to get by in retirement on social security, and maybe, they are even thinking about continuing to work well into their 70s.

That paints a grim picture, especially when you consider that simply following a few rules can help you build amazing levels of wealth over time. The reality is that it's definitely better if you start investing when you're young, and I hope that at least some readers are still in their 20s and 30s and are looking for ways to build up some wealth so they can at least be secure in their retirement, and who knows, many will be able to retire early and live off the income that dividend investments can provide.

However, all is not lost. Even if you are 50, 60, or even older, it's never too late to do something. In this chapter, I would like to discuss a few ways for you to accelerate your investments so that you don't have to get by eating cat food in your retirement years.

If you don't have a retirement account open an IRA

You can open a traditional IRA all the way until age 70 ½. You can only invest $6,500 a year if you are over age 50, but remember that every little bit counts and you can build up a little nest egg over time that can add to your income from social security. You should open one as soon as possible if you are age 50 or over and you don't have any savings or investments. The maximum you can invest is $6,500 a year, and that is only $542 a month. For some people, that will be a big expense, but how big is it going to be when you are 75 years old and have no income at all besides a small social security payment? If you have to take on a second job or do something like drive for Uber or deliver for Door Dash, you need to start doing it now and get that extra $542 and invest it every single month. If you start buying dividend stocks now, then 20 years from now, you will be able to earn some income from them and avoid complete poverty. Also, remember the trick I provided about taxes and using an IRA account, you can grow your account faster than imagined by just investing $6,500 a year by selling covered calls and reinvesting your dividends.

Find ways to earn more income and invest it

I hate to sound too repetitive, but the modern economy provides many ways to earn extra money. You should take up as many gigs as you can. If you have no savings and investment, you need to do it and get going on this now. Take the money you earn from a second job or from gigs and use it not only to fund an IRA but to start building the kind of dividend plan that we've described in this book.

Buy and Sell Options

Buying and selling options is a good way to start profiting from the stock market because you can start small. However, a word of caution – profiting from options is a little bit tricky. Don't just go out and start doing it. You need to read books and take a course or two to really learn how to do it properly. What I am talking about here is different than what we discussed about options earlier in the book. I am suggesting that you put some time in to become an options trader, not using your stocks to sell covered calls (but you can do that too, and you should be doing it if you are low on your investments and need to raise more cash, but own some shares). Trading options can begin one contract at a time, investing in amounts of $50, $100, or more. Think long term and do it carefully. You are going to have some losses, but if you follow the advice outlined here, and take some courses, your odds of having far more wins will be significantly increased. The only other thing to say here is don't go all in on options, do small amounts each month, say a few hundred dollars. If you can get to where you invest $500 and come out with $1,000 in many months, then you can take your profits and invest them in dividend stocks. Options are a low-cost way to start accelerating the investment plans that you should have started years ago.

Have a regular dividend stock plan

Develop a plan to start buying solid dividend stocks at a level that you can afford. Make it a plan that you're not going to avoid carrying out because you're faced with buying a few shares or paying the electric bill. Once you settle on a plan, carry it out and don't deviate. The only change should be increasing your stock purchases when you can afford it.

Don't cheat yourself with early withdrawals

If you are not financially secure, the temptation will be there to pull money out of your investments and spend it now. That is a huge mistake; you're actually throwing away large sums of money that you would earn if you left the money invested. If you find yourself needing extra money, find another way to get it.

Conclusion

Thanks for finishing this book and taking the time to read it. I am hopeful that you enjoyed the book and found it informative.

Investing in the stock market can be very exciting and lucrative. If done correctly, you can use your investments in the stock market over time to grow your wealth and after a number of years; you can earn a significant living from dividends alone. Take your time and evaluate each investment before putting your money in, so that you don't end up wasting it.

CPSIA information can be obtained
at www.ICGtesting.com
Printed in the USA
LVHW050402210621
690710LV00010B/1002